D1560176

Work-Family Role Choices for Women in Their 20s and 30s

Work-Family Role Choices for Women in Their 20s and 30s

From College Plans to Life Experiences

Cherlyn Skromme Granrose
Eileen E. Kaplan

Westport, Connecticut
London

Library of Congress Cataloging-in-Publication Data

Granrose, Cherlyn S.
    Work-family role choices for women in their 20s and 30s : from college plans to
life experiences / Cherlyn Skromme Granrose, Eileen E. Kaplan.
        p.   cm.
    Includes bibliographical references and index.
    ISBN 0–275–95525–7 (alk. paper)
    1. Working mothers—United States—Longitudinal studies.   2. Women
college graduates—United States—Longitudinal studies.   3. Work and
family—United States—Longitudinal studies.   4. Women—Employment—
United States—Decision making—Longitudinal studies.   I. Kaplan,
Eileen E.   II. Title.
HQ759.48.G73   1996
306.874′3—dc20   96–2195

British Library Cataloguing in Publication Data is available.

Library of Congress Catalog Card Number: 96–2195
ISBN: 0–275–95525–7

First published in 1996

Praeger Publishers, 88 Post Road West, Westport, CT 06881
An imprint of Greenwood Publishing Group, Inc.

Printed in the United States of America

The paper used in this book complies with the
Permanent Paper Standard issued by the National
Information Standards Organization (Z39.48–1984).

10 9 8 7 6 5 4 3 2

This book is dedicated to our families—Karen, Paul, Andrew, and Jack Kaplan; and Karen Friend, Kathleen, and Jonathan Granrose—to our students, and to the wonderful women who participated in this study. May your particular ways of combining employment and family responsibilities bring you great joy!

E.E.K. and C.S.G.

Contents

Tables

Preface

Combining employment roles and family roles is one of the crucial challenges most men and women face in the twenty-first century. Yet society is changing so rapidly because of advances in technology, increased social diversity, and greater global competition, that advice from well-meaning friends, relatives, and mentors may no longer be accurate. We want to provide an empirically based record of the real experiences of women facing this challenge today. We wrote this book primarily to provide sound information to young adult women, their friends, spouses, employers, and counselors. The information is based on a 10-year longitudinal study of college graduate women. It is presented in narrative form, rather than a scientific format, to encourage nonscientists to use the results in their daily life choices.

Like many longitudinal studies, there were issues we wanted to address in the 1990s that hadn't seemed so important in the 1980s. In 1980, asking women whether or not they would return to work during the first three years following childbirth seemed logical. That was when most day care centers took children and the years when a large number of women returned to employment if they were going to be employed mothers. Today, we wished we had asked about returning to work after a shorter period, but we did the best we could to understand 1990s reality by asking more detailed questions in the followup questionnaire. Given these longitudinal limitations, the voices of the women who participated in this study still emerge today as one of a handful of written records of how women cope with multiple roles and how they feel about the choices they have made.

The empirical project used as a foundation for this book was unusual as social science research goes, in that we did not have a great deal of trouble getting women to participate when their names came up in the random sampling procedure. Through generous assistance from the Rutgers University and Temple University Alumnae Associations, as well as from families and friends, we were able to trace what happened to women in the first decade after college graduation, and we got a good response from those we found. Notes written on questionnaires told us that women were willing to be cooperative in filling out long questionnaires because they were interested in the topic and hoped their participation would help themselves and others grapple with these complicated life choices.

In return, we wanted to convey their thoughts and feelings as accurately as possible without betraying the confidentiality of the respondents. As a result, pseudonyms have been used throughout, and some quotes have been edited or combined with another response to protect a respondent's privacy, or combined with the original question to provide an intelligible sentence. However, every quote is based on actual responses and did not come from the authors' imaginations.

In addition to using many quotes to let women speak in their own voices, we also wanted to make the quantitative analyses of the responses interesting to read. Therefore, a minimum number of tables comparing each group's responses from the 1980s to their responses in the 1990s are included in the text. The actual questionnaires and more complicated tables comparing responses across groups of women are located in the Appendix.

In addition, we chose to highlight in the text the significant differences that were important for each group of women and that were consistent with telephone interviews, rather than presenting long, dry, lists of every single significant difference between groups. While this may inconvenience some academic readers, the relevant statistical data to substantiate all significant group differences are presented in the tables. We hope this format will be less confusing to the nonacademic women reading this book. Scholars wishing additional empirical information may find it published in traditional academic journals or may request more information from the authors.

When this project started in the early 1980s, both of us were pursuing graduate degrees while raising children, and both of us wrote dissertations about adult women's life decisions. When it came time to do a follow-up study, we decided to collaborate because of our common interest in how women's lives change over time. The 1980 survey data were collected by Cherry Granrose, while the 1990 survey data were collected collaboratively.

Finally, the 1990 telephone interviews used to enrich our understanding of the data were supervised by Eileen Kaplan. Each of us took responsibility for writing the first draft of specific chapters then edited each other's work. The resulting manuscript is a collaboration that reflects both of our perspectives rather than any one author's opinion.

One difficulty we encountered when writing about this topic concerns the word "work." We have tried to use the terms "employment" or "paid" work" to refer to work done for money, usually outside of the home. Sometimes we also use the single word "work" to refer to this circumstance. This in no way implies that we do not recognize that child care and homemaking are not socially valuable and challenging work. Rather, we hope readers see that we value all roles and try to identify the location of work in places where it might be unclear.

We could not have completed this long project without the help of innumerable graduate students and tireless typists. In particular, Rama Devi was crucial in doing the longitudinal data analyses; B. J. Reich and Jane Gray typed the final draft of the manuscript. We appreciate their help and support at times when this project seemed interminable.

We hope this book provides information you find helpful and welcome your comments in writing or on the Internet.

Cherlyn Skromme Granrose
Center for Organizational and Behavioral Sciences
Claremont Graduate School
Claremont, California 91711
GRANROSC@CGS.EDU

Eileen E. Kaplan
Department of Management
Montclair State University
Upper Montclair, NJ 07043
KAPLANE@SATURN.MONTCLAIR.EDU

Work-Family Role Choices
for Women in
Their 20s and 30s

Chapter 1

Sources of Ambiguity in Women's Development: The Context

I always planned to return to work after having a baby. After spending four and a half years working on my MBA and advancing my career very rapidly in a male-dominated organization, I did not feel ready to throw everything away or put it on the shelf. We liked the financial security of two incomes. But after four months of 60-hour weeks, two baby sitters, one totaled automobile (by a baby sitter), and extreme levels of stress and guilt, I decided my son was more important and left my job. (Anna)

Anna's ambivalence reflects the difficult choices facing many college-educated American women. As women come of age today, they encounter critical family and employment decisions filled with ambiguity. The struggle with ambiguity particularly characterizes their choices of whether or not to return to paid work after having children.

This volume explores the relationship between career and family plans made by a group of college women in the early 1980s and their subsequent decisions about returning to paid work after the birth of their first child in the 1990s. It looks at some of the forces creating ambiguity and ambivalence, then relates how this group of women made their choices and evaluated the consequences.

In examining the way women make these choices, we address the following questions:

- What are the models or metaphors used to explain how young adults change?

- When in college, how do women plan to combine paid work and family roles?
- What impact do post-college experiences with employment, personal relationships, and motherhood have on women's decisions?
- How consistent are women's career plans with their eventual decisions about returning to paid work after the birth of their children?
- What do these experiences suggest for women as well as for employing organizations?

To begin to answer these questions, we first explore two explanations for what happens as women pass through their twenties and enter their thirties. Next we describe important social changes occurring in the United States today as young women move from childhood to adulthood. Succeeding chapters give specific examples of the process by which one small but strategic group of women made decisions about returning to paid work after childbirth, the factors that facilitated or constrained their decisions, and the consequences of each alternative they believe are important.

MODELS OF MATURATION

Young adults today are growing up in a social climate that reflects enormous changes in identity and gender roles.[1] For many, the traditional "mom and pop" picture no longer reflects reality. Models of psychological development in adulthood describe and explain these changes and help us interpret what we see.

There are two major frameworks for viewing adult developmental changes. The first framework describes changes as a function of chronological age or stages. Age-based theories and descriptions of adult changes generally emphasize the maturational aspects of adult development. Thus, proponents view development as a sequence of stages, each associated with developing competence in mastering unique themes, tasks, and difficulties.

The second framework describes changes as a function of socialization to roles in response to historical events. Social role-based descriptions of adult changes emphasize the impact of social change on development. Proponents of this view see adult development as occurring in a smooth continuum influenced by changing social norms and historical events. Both frameworks have something to contribute to an explanation of how young women move from college into family and professional adult lives.

Stage Approaches to Individual Development

Life stage approaches to adulthood conceive of the lifespan as a linear progression through various age-related stages of development. Each stage contains a set of developmental tasks and concerns that must be addressed. A person moves through these stages striving to complete these tasks competently and then attends to a new set of tasks. Models based on this viewpoint seek to identify the differing stages of adulthood and the characteristics that represent successful and less successful passage through these stages.

Much of this view is shaped by the work of Erik Erikson.[2] He described young men moving from late childhood to early adulthood as striving to achieve a sense of self-definition. Self-definition not only gives a sense of knowing where they are going, but also meets with support and approval from significant others in their lives. According to Erikson, attaining a sense of inner identity, the developmental task of young adulthood, represents the ability to adapt special skills, capacities, and strengths to the prevailing role structure of society. Erikson also believed that successfully completing the life tasks of a particular stage fosters a strong sense of self or "identity." If this sense of self is positively evaluated by the individual and others, it contributes to both a sense of competence and self-esteem.

To apply Erikson's ideas to women's development, given today's role definitions, young women must actively consider involvement in both occupational and family roles in adulthood. This perspective suggests that how women define their life tasks and how others evaluate both the appropriateness of their choice of tasks and their competence in accomplishing these tasks are critical factors defining women's passage from their early 20s to their early 30s. For many women in our study, a major task is determining how to combine these roles to give them a sense of identity based on feelings of competence and self-esteem.

Levinson et al.[3] proposed another stage-based view of adult development. They demonstrated that adult men and women move through alternating developmental and transitional periods in the life cycle. Each developmental period presents tasks to be mastered and problems to be solved. Major tasks of these developmental periods include making crucial choices, creating a structure around them, enriching the structure, and pursuing one's goals within it. Between each developmental period are transition periods that allow individuals to question who they are and where they want to go. The major tasks of these transition periods are to reexamine need and value hierarchies; to take another look at various life components, such as occupations and relationships; to explore and evaluate potential options; and to make decisions to either deepen or alter earlier commitments. Levinson proposed that one such transition period occurs around age 30.

Because both Erikson and Levinson originally explored their stage theories only among men and then later adapted their findings to include women, less is known about adult development of young women than of young men. Some developmental scholars suggest that the lives of women follow different patterns than those of men; while men's lives are guided by autonomy and individuation, women's lives are guided by attachment and care. Others suggest that women go through the same stages as men but that the issues and timing differ.[4] For example, at about age 30, both sexes perceive themselves as reassessing their lives and seeking some unknown changes, but the nature of the change may differ.

Reinke et al.[5] provide some evidence that women start a period of major psychosocial transition between the ages of 27 and 30. This transition is characterized initially by personal disruption, followed by reassessment and a search for personal growth, and finally a spurt in self-concept and psychological well-being. For women with employment careers, these thoughts may center on having a child, whereas women who have stayed home with young children may entertain thoughts of returning to the paid labor force. Inner biological maturational processes may be involved in this transition, and perhaps the age 30 marker has been imbued with societal significance for women as well as men.

Stage-based explanations of how women change tend to minimize all but immediate social contacts in the surrounding social setting. Others insist that broader social changes cannot be ignored when trying to explain how adults develop and change.

Social Change and Development

Those who emphasize the socio-cultural context of personal development suggest that major social and historical events during childhood affect an individual's broad values and expectations about the world.[6] Carol Gilligan[7] and others also suggest that girls and boys go through different socialization experiences in our society. Boys are encouraged to value autonomy and achievement, girls are rewarded for developing nurturant relationships.

Historical events occurring in late adolescence and young adulthood also are likely to influence beliefs and assumptions about the way the world does, and should, work. Since young adults already have formed world views and values, new events may be assimilated into these preexisting views if they are consistent. If they are very discrepant, however, specific events may cause a shift in these views to accommodate social changes. For example, returning WWII veterans needing jobs stimulated many women who had worked during the war to become homemakers. Thus, historical events helped shape attitudes and norms about working mothers in the 1950s and 1960s. Post–Vietnam-war cultural and economic changes in the 1970s again changed norms about maternal work. As norms change, so do patterns of childhood socialization about values and expectations. Changing customs of socializing men and women are one source of ambiguity women face as they develop in their 20s. Social events also can influence adolescents' and young adults' opportunities and life choices that forge adult identities.

In the view of many, women still are predisposed to enter nurturing relationships and seek to achieve an identity based on competency through interpersonal relationships and taking care of others. Other researchers believe that identities based on competence now derive from successfully combining paid work and family.[8]

Scholars attempting to integrate both perspectives about how women change in early adulthood point to the common developmental life tasks of deciding how to economically support oneself after leaving a parental family and how to begin to create a new family.[9] They also examine the social context in which women decide how to accomplish these tasks. Biologically driven desires to start a family or socially determined financial pressures to take a job outside of the home suggest that both models of adult development have something to offer. Although some changes may be related to chronological age, it is likely that social environment factors in addition to maturational factors may be responsible for age-related patterns. Since the women described in this book are facing these developmental tasks in a time of rapid social change, we look first at the social context of their maturation and then describe their individual lives and choices made within this context.

SOURCES OF AMBIGUITY IN THE CHANGING SOCIAL SETTING

Because each decade since the women described in this book were born involved substantial social change, the participants made life-shaping decisions in a context full of mixed messages and fragmented, differing, subcultures. Key sources of ambiguity in the environment include changing social structures, changing attitudes and values, and new educational and employment opportunities for women.

Changing Social Structure

The dramatic changes in social behavior and attitudes during the past three decades stimulate much of the ambiguity women face today. They include a decline in full-time mothering, a rise in women working for pay, and an increased need for families to have two incomes to maintain a sense of material well-being.[10]

In her book, *Hard Choices*, Kathleen Gerson argues that female domesticity during the post–World War II years depended upon the reinforcing effects of certain social arrangements: permanent, stable marriages; households founded on male breadwinners; limited work opportunities for women; and sufficient behavioral similarity among women to support traditional norms.[11] In response, the vast majority of women eschewed the workplace in favor of the homemaker role; those who did not were subject to pity.

But even as female domesticity predominated, its underpinnings were beginning to erode. Starting around the mid-1960s and early 1970s, expanded opportunities in the workplace quickened the pace of change and dramatically altered the forces women faced outside the home.[12] For many couples, a second income became necessary to provide the desired standard of living. As more women obtained college degrees, they secured better jobs and worked more years in a wider variety of nondomestic fields.

In response to these changes, fewer women pursued full-time careers as homemakers. Although labor force participation has increased among women of all ages, it is particularly striking among women of prime childbearing age. As Table 1.1 indicates, in 1970 approximately one-third of all women with children under three worked for pay. By 1980, that number had increased to about 42 percent. More than half of the mothers of young children were employed by 1990.[13]

The general consensus of the nature of this social change is that, in some ways, the roles of both sexes have become more similar: Men are more involved in the family; women have taken on an increasing share of the breadwinner role. Yet recent evidence suggests that changes within the home have been small while changes in women's employment have been great.[14] Although married men spend more time in child care and food preparation, such participation is primarily limited to weekends.[15] Even wives with full-time professional careers take care of the majority of domestic tasks involving day-to-day survival of the household. Thus, women have experienced only modest changes in the actual division of labor within the family.

Table 1.1
Three Decades of Employment of Women

	1970	1980	1990
% of women employed	43.3	51.5	57.5
% white	42.6	51.2	52.0
% black/other	49.5	53.1	32.2
% of mothers employed			
Children under 18	42.2	46.0	66.6
Children under 8	30.3	45.1	---
Children under 6	23.0	45.0	58.2
Children under 3	34.3	41.9	53.6

Source: Statistical Abstract of the United States, 1992; Department of Commerce, Bureau of Census.

A possible consequence of this asymmetrical change is role overload. Thus, a number of scholarly studies emphasize the many stresses and strains women experience as a result of this shift. When women opt for careers of employment, they add paid work roles and demands to their lives without decreasing traditional family expectations. But other studies find that combining family and employment contributes to women's happiness.[16] Some women report synergistic experiences in which family experiences enrich employment and vice versa.

Women who choose full-time domesticity also encounter new pressures. By not engaging in employment, some women worry because they are out of step with changes in gender norms. Research suggests that homemakers experience as much, or more, distress later in life than their counterparts who resumed employment after childbirth.[17]

This combination of potential synergy and potential stress surrounding either choice increases the ambiguity of young women's choices. One way women may respond to such ambiguity is to examine their values to help them make decisions. But values and norms also have changed.

Changing Gender Roles

By the late 1970s, changes in gender role norms and related social values were particularly evident in young people.[18] Young adults had more egalitarian attitudes toward new roles for men and women than did older adults.

In a recent attitudinal survey of 200,000 United States college students, the American Council on Higher Education reports that more than 90 percent agree with the statement that "women should receive the same salaries and career opportunities as men in comparable positions." Three-quarters disagree with the statement that "the activities of married women are best confined to the home and family."[19] A number of studies indicate that both young men and women are moving away from a belief in the traditionally defined separate roles for men and women.

Nevertheless, many young adults seem torn between traditional views and new roles for both women and men.[20] Not surprisingly, women are more likely than men to express a desire for equality in their work and family relationships.[21] Yet, not all women share a common attitude toward employment careers. Despite declines in normative support for full-time mothering, some young women continue to support the traditional homemaker role. Others hold egalitarian professional views but have more traditional expectations for their own relationships and future partners than they do for women in general.

One study of six universities around the United States reported that more than nine out of ten students considered themselves "highly" or "moderately" career-oriented in 1986. Virtually all of the men and more than 90 percent of the women said they planned to work full time for most of their lives. Yet more than 80 percent said they planned to have children. (Only five percent said they *definitely would not* become parents.) While most students believed that a woman should bear her first child between the ages of 22 and 30, they had few plans for parental leave. The students assumed that someone—more likely the female—would interrupt an employment career, but they did not seem aware of potential negative career or financial consequences. Furthermore, women respondents had somewhat unrealistic views about the workplace and did not see a link between taking time off for child care and lack of career advancement.[22]

Changing Higher Education Opportunities

While changes in attitudes toward women who combine paid work and family caretaking are linked to the amount and type of education women receive, education itself creates more ambiguity. As women increasingly invest time and money in their college and professional education, they become less likely to turn away from a future that uses their skills.

The number of women earning advanced college degrees as well as degrees from professional schools is at an all time high (see Table 1.2).[23] This trend is accompanied by a shift in the major fields of study women

Table 1.2
Trends in the Educational Attainment of Women

Degrees Conferred			
% Female	1970	1980	1990
Bachelor's	45	49	56
Master's	40	49	51
Doctor's	10	30	36

Source: Digest of Education Statistics, annual; U.S. National Center for Education Statistics.

choose. For example, the percentage of women who say they plan business careers has increased dramatically. Majors such as computer science and engineering have become more popular while enrollments of women in majors such as education have declined.[24]

Even more striking is the change in the percentage of graduate degrees conferred on women in selected professions. By 1986, women received 31 percent of the MBA degrees, a 500 percent increase in just a little over a decade. Women also received 30 percent, 39 percent, and 22.6 percent of all medical, law, and dentistry degrees, respectively.[25] Such shifts signal commitment to a career orientation tied less to traditional nurturing concerns and more to employment to achieve financial and status goals.

Changing Employment Experiences

Just as changes in educational opportunities have increased ambiguity, so have new employment experiences. In the past two decades, four specific changes in women's experiences on the job provide clues to the variety of new experiences facing women. First, more women have moved from limited paid work before and after family life to full-time, long-term attachment to the labor force. Second, paralleling their educational gains, women increasingly have moved into managerial and professional positions. While still a distinct minority in many traditionally male occupations, their representation between the mid-1970s and the 1990s has increased substantially. Third, women have found that advancement opportunities, although fairly abundant at lower levels of an organization, became increasingly constricted, often in a discriminatory way, at more senior levels. Finally, the large-scale entry of women into corporate America coincided with a period of continuous restructuring and downsizing.

Research evidence indicates that future paid work behavior is best predicted not by attitudes or values but by past employment. The longer a woman works before childbirth, the more likely she is to remain in the labor force on a continuous basis following the birth of a child.[26] A longer employment history provides opportunities to earn more money, to develop new skills, to get more interesting assignments, and to develop job contacts that in turn lead to appealing opportunities. Since more women are delaying childbirth and experiencing longer prechildbirth work histories, these opportunities are more available to them if they choose to return to paid work following childbirth.

The occupational distribution of women in the labor force reflects expanding opportunities for women (see Table 1.3). In the past, the vast majority of women clustered into a few traditionally female service occupations (nursing, education, social work). During the last two decades, however, they have been entering occupations that offer more status, higher pay, and more job opportunities (for examples managers, engineers, systems analysts.)[27]

Entering a formerly predominantly male field does not guarantee advancement, however. Explanations for women's lack of career advancement vary. Some human capital theory academicians contend that women do not advance into senior levels of an organization because large numbers of women have not been in the labor force long enough to be in the pipeline for these positions.[28] This argument is increasingly weak in the 1990s, however.

Others attribute women's lack of advancement in organizations to a "glass ceiling" effect. In this view, women are likely to "bump" against a transparent barrier that prevents them from rising above a certain level.[29] A fair amount of evidence exists that men and women at middle and senior

Table 1.3
Trends in Occupations

Occupation % Female	1970	1980	1990
Managerial/Professional	33.9	40.6	46.5
Technical, Sales, Admin. Support	59.0	64.4	64.3
Service Occupations	59.7	58.9	60.0

Source: U.S. Department of Labor, Bureau of Labor Statistics, Employment and Earnings, January 1991, *38*(1).

levels exhibit similar aspirations, values, personal characteristics, job-related skills, and behaviors.[30] These findings imply that it is not a deficiency on the part of female candidates that holds them back from top positions; instead, it is attitudinal and structural discrimination practiced by the dominant group of men.[31]

One subtle form of discrimination may be conflicting expectations about appropriate gender role behavior at senior levels—"Should one behave as a woman with 'feminine' characteristics or as an executive with characteristics synonymous with traditional male gender roles?" Recent research continues to indicate that a "good" manager is described as "masculine" rather than as "androgynous," particularly by male managers and executives. In fact, being able to walk that fine line by combining acceptably "masculine" and "feminine" behaviors might count for more than performance on the job when advancement decisions are made.[32]

The case of *Hopkins v. Price Waterhouse* illustrates how implicit expectations become explicit forms of discrimination.[33] Ms. Hopkins was denied a partnership in a Big Six accounting firm based not on her performance but on her behavior, which was considered unacceptably masculine by the executive committee. She was eventually awarded the partnership (and retroactive pay) when the United States Supreme Court ruled in her favor on the grounds that she had been denied the promotion on the basis of sex discrimination.

Other forms of discrimination also apply. Women who are potential executive candidates are likely to be looked at with misgivings if anyone or anything is thought to interfere with their total commitment to their careers. In fact, women executives are more likely to be childless or to have fewer children than either their male counterparts or women at other levels of the organization. In some cases this is a response to heavy career expectations and conflicts between differences in expectations for parental roles between men and women.[34]

Some organizations try to relieve this pressure in ways that are controversial. They have proposed to formally inaugurate a double track system: Early in their careers women would be identified as "career primary" (those following a male career model and presumably not having children) or "career and family" (those following a so-called "mommy track," whereby they would sacrifice career potential to spend more time with their families).[35]

Such schemes, well-intentioned as they may be, send a clear message to women about the strains and the sacrifices needed to reach upper levels in an organization and the inappropriateness of "executive mothers." Such messages may be one reason why some young women become disillusioned and reluctant to engage in career planning. One look at the organizational landscape signals to them that combining career advancement and having children may be very difficult, if not impossible. Women and men more supportive of humane workplaces and gender role equality suggest that organizations should restructure paid work and provide family care to enable both men and women to enact parental *and* employee roles effectively.

In addition to discrimination, economic factors are affecting women's employment opportunities. In the past decade, women have witnessed increased demand for productivity and innovation in an uncertain, rapidly changing global environment. Such changes frequently resulted in organizational structures with fewer levels of management and decentralized decision making with increased control of output and process.[36] A number of women and men have lost their jobs through massive layoffs or been shifted to temporary or part-time positions with limited or no fringe benefits. Job security—formerly a key advantage in working for a large organization—was reduced, if not eliminated. As a result, many women either started their own businesses or took jobs in smaller companies—alternatives that were less likely to offer the family benefits (child care, parental leave) found in larger organizations.

The opportunity structure within most organizations changed dramatically. Just as women made their greatest progress into middle management jobs, these jobs were cut back. As one woman manager explained, "When organizations flatten, it limits the number of rungs on the ladder, which lengthens the time between promotions."[37] Not only did cuts of the eighties and nineties make career planning more difficult, they also made planning more important than ever.

Another outcome of downsizing was that so-called survivors often wound up doing more than one job.[38] Having an increased number of jobs to do required greater self-management and technological know-how but brought little increase in salaries. Concomitant with this change, predictable and regular work hours became increasingly rare, making it more difficult to combine paid work and family responsibilities.

In summary, by the mid-1990s, expanding educational and organizational opportunities enabled more women to work outside the home in a wider range of jobs. But paid work was less enjoyable, more pressured, and provided less opportunity to advance.

Although these changes indicate that women are entering employment careers that require strong commitment to paid work, the potential impact of these shifts on women's careers provokes serious debate.

To some, organizations seem as antiwomen and as unchanged as ever. To others, the rigid structures appear to be starting to give way to greater flexibility and more policies supporting working families. To some, exhausting 60-hour weeks brought about by endless cost cutting and restructuring make any rational plans for combining paid work and family impossible. To others, it seems that companies are finally beginning to recognize the need to accommodate employed parents. Some reports allege that women are leaving organizations to care for their children, and perhaps start their own businesses.[39] Others claim these reports are exaggerated and this phenomenon is not occurring to any great extent. To some, the "mommy track" is the perfect solution to the dilemma of how to combine employment and family; to others, it merely sets back women's progress in organizations. Some indicate that women in nontraditional (i.e., predominantly male) occupations are having a tougher time than their counterparts in traditionally female occupations. But others point out that their earnings are higher and that they have more opportunity to advance than in the past.

The ambiguity in perceptions of changing social structures, gender role norms, and organizations creates a confusing environment for women to decide how much of their lives to devote to employment and how much to devote to childrearing. In the following chapters of this book we will show that the extent to which women link their identities to the homemaker and paid worker roles has a large impact on the way they respond to these ambiguities.

In the face of conflicting and unclear environmental signals, those who adopted an ideology that contained beliefs affirming their own self-concept exhibited remarkably stable life plans and behavior. Those who did not link their identity to a particular role choice responded to social trends and beliefs that often changed their plans.

NOTES

1. P. Voydonoff. (1988). Work and family: A review and expanded conceptualization. *Journal of Social Behavior and Personality, 3*, 1–22.

2. E. Erikson. (1950). *Childhood and society*. New York: Norton. 1980; E. Erikson. (1980). *Identity and the life cycle*. New York: Norton; E. Morgan & B. A. Farber. (1982). Toward a re-formulation of the Ericksonian model of female identity development. *Adolescence, 17*, 199–211.

3. D. J. Levinson, C. N. Darrow, E. B. Klein, M. Levinson, & B. McKee. (1978). *The seasons of a man's life*. New York: Knopf.

4. S. Ornstein & L. Isabella. (1990). Age vs. stage models of career attitudes of women: A partial replication and extension. *Journal of Vocational Behavior, 36*, 1–19.

5. B. J. Reinke, D. S. Holmes, & R. L. Harris. (1985). The timing of psychosocial changes in women's lives: The years 25 to 45. *Journal of Personality and Social Psychology*, *48*, 1353–1364.

6. A. J. Stewart & J. M. Healy, Jr. (1989). Linking individual development and social changes. *American Psychologist, 44*, 30–42; G. Powell & L. Mainiero. (1992). Crosscurrents in the river of time: Conceptualizing the complexities of women's careers. *Journal of Management, 18*, 215–237.

7. C. Gilligan. (1979). Woman's place in a man's life cycle. *Harvard Educational Review, 49*, 431–446; C. Gilligan. (1982). *In a different voice*: *Psychological theory and women's development*. Cambridge, MA: Harvard University Press.

8. B. A. Gutek & L. Larwood (Eds.). (1986). *Women's career development*. Newbury Park, CA: Sage.

9. B. A. Gutek & L. Larwood (Eds.). (1986). *Women's career development*. Newbury Park, CA: Sage.

10. G. Powell & L. Mainiero. (1992). Crosscurrents in the river of time: Conceptualizing the complexities of women's careers. *Journal of Management, 18*, 215–237.

11. K. Gerson. (1985). *Hard choices: How women decide about work, career and motherhood*. Berkeley: University of California Press.

12. C. Rexroat. (1992). Changes in the employment continuity of succeeding cohorts of young women. *Work and Occupations, 19*, 18–34,12.

13. *Outlook 2000*. (1990). Washington, DC: Bureau of Labor Statistics, Office of Employment Projections.

14. S. Coverman. (1985). Explaining husbands' participation in domestic labor. *Sociological Quarterly, 26*, 81–97; J. D. Fox & S. Nichols. (1983). The time crunch. *Journal of Family Issues, 4*, 61–82; M. Geerken & W. R. Grove. (1983). *At home and at work*. Beverly Hills, CA: Sage; G. Spitz. (1986). The division of task responsibility in U.S. households: Longitudinal adjustments to change. *Social Forces, 65*, 671–689.

15. S. F. Berk. (1985). *The gender factory: The apportionment of work in American households*. New York: Plenum; G. Farkas. (1976). Education, wage rates and the division of labor between husband and wife. *Journal of Marriage and the Family, 39*, 473–483; I. McAllister. (1990). Gender and the household division of labor. *Work and Occupations, 17*, 79–99.

16. G. K. Baruch & R. Barnett. (1986). Role quality, multiple role involvement, and psychological well-being among midlife women. *Journal of Personality and Social Psychology, 51*, 578–585; J. H. Greenhaus. (1989). Intersection of work and family roles. In E. B. Goldsmith (Ed.), *Work and family—Theory, research and applications*. Newbury Park, CA: Sage; N. Kibria, R. C. Barnett, G. K. Baruch, N. L. Marshall, & J. H. Pleck. (1990). Homemaking role quality and the psychological well-being and distress of employed women. *Sex Roles, 22*, 327–347; P. Voydanoff & B. W. Donnelly. (1989). Work and family roles and psychological distress. *Journal of Marriage and the Family, 51*, 923–932; F. Crosby. (1991). *Juggling: The unexpected advantage of balancing career and*

home for women and their families. New York: The Free Press; C. Kirchmeyer. (1993). Nonwork-to-work spillover: A more balanced view of the experiences and coping of professional women and men. *Sex Roles, 28*, 531–552.

17. R. Helson & J. Picano. (1990). Is the traditional role bad for women? *Journal of Personality and Social Psychology, 59*, 311–320.

18. L. B. Lueptow. (1985). Conceptions of femininity and masculinity: 1974–1983. *Psychological Reports, 57*, 859–862.

19. A. Astin. (1990). *The American freshman: National norms for fall 1989.* Los Angeles: UCLA, American Council on Education.

20. Attitudes and characteristics. *Chronicle of Higher Education*, September 5, 1990, p. 14.

21. T. J. Covin & C. C. Brush. (1991). An examination of male and female attitudes toward career and family issues. *Sex Roles, 25*, 393–415.

22. *Survey of college student attitudes in six U.S. colleges and universities.* (1986). New York: Catalyst.

23. *Statistical Abstract of the United States: 1990* (110th edition). Washington, DC: U.S. Bureau of the Census, p. 161.

24. A. W. Astin, K. C. Green, & W. S. Korn. (1986). *The American freshman: Twenty year trends.* Los Angeles; UCLA Cooperative Institutional Research Program, American Council on Education,

25. Sara E. Rix (Ed.). (1990). *The American woman 1988–89: A status report.* New York: W. W. Norton & Co.

26. S. D. McLaughlin. (1982). Differential patterns of female labor-force participation surrounding the first birth. *Journal of Marriage and the Family, 44*, 407–420; C. Rexroat & C. Shehan. (1984). Expected versus actual work roles of women. *American Sociological Review, 49*, 349–358.

27. *Statistical Abstract of the United States: 1990* (110th edition). Washington, DC; U.S. Bureau of the Census, pp. 389–390; S. S. Tangri & S. R. Jenkins. (1986). Stability and change in role innovation and life plans. *Sex Roles, 14*, 647–662.

28. M. McComas. (1986, April 28). Atop the Fortune 500: A survey of CEOs. *Fortune*, 26–31.

29. U.S. Department of Labor. (1991). *A report on the glass ceiling initiative.* Washington, DC: U.S. Department of Labor, Lynn Martin, Secretary; L. K. Stroh, J. M. Brett, & A. H. Reilly. (1992). All the right stuff: A comparison of female and male managers' career progression. *Journal of Applied Psychology, 77*, 251–260.

30. A. M. Morrison, R. P. White, & E. V. Van Velsor. (1987). *Breaking the glass ceiling: Can women reach the top of America's largest corporations?* Reading, MA: Addison Wesley; G. H. Dobbins & S. J. Platz. (1986). Sex differences in leadership: How real are they? *Academy of Management Review, 11*, 118–127; S. M. Donnell & J. Hall. (1980). Men and women as managers: A significant case of no significant difference. *Organizational Dynamics, 8*, 60–76; A. Harlan & C. Weiss. (1981). *Moving up: Women in managerial careers.* Working paper no. 86. Wellesley, MA: Wellesley College; A. M. Morrison & M. A.

VonGlinow. (1990). Women and minorities in management. *American Psychologist*, *45*, 200–208.

31. A. M. Morrison, R. P. White, & E. V. Van Velsor. (1987). *Breaking the glass ceiling: Can women reach the top of America's largest corporations?* Reading, MA: Addison Wesley.

32. O. C. Brenner, J. Tomkiewicz, & V. E. Schein. (1989). The relationship between sex role stereotypes and requisite management characteristics revisited. *Academy of Management Journal*, *32*, 662–669; G. N. Powell & D. A. Butterfield. (1989). The "good manager": Did androgyny fare better in the 1980s? *Group and Organization Studies*, *14*, 216–233.

33. Big eight accounting firms found to be still a male bastion. *New York Times*, July 12, 1988.

34. J. Fierman. (1990, July 30). Why women still don't hit the top. *Fortune*, 40–62.

35. F. Schwartz. (1989, Jan.–Feb.). Management women and the new facts of life. *Harvard Business Review*, 65–76.

36. P. F. Drucker. (1988, Jan.–Feb.). The coming of the new organization. *Harvard Business Review*, 65–76; R. M. Kanter. (1989, Nov.–Dec.). The new managerial work. *Harvard Business Review*, 85–92; T. A. Kochan, J. P. Macduffie, & P. Osterman. (1988). Employment security at DEC: Sustaining values amid environmental change. *Human Resource Management*, *27*, 121–143.

37. D. Kirkpatrick. (1990, July 2). Is your career on track? *Fortune*, 38–48.

38. J. Brockner, S. Grover, & M. Blonder. (1988). Predictors of survivors' job involvement following layoffs: A field study. *Journal of Applied Psychology*, *73*, 436–442; T. D. Jick. (1985). As the ax falls: Budget cuts and the experience of stress in organizations. In T. A. Beehr & R. S. Bhagat (Eds.), *Human stress and cognition in organizations.* New York: Wiley; M. West, N. Nicholson, & A. Rees. (1990). The outcomes of downward managerial mobility. *Journal of Organizational Behavior*, *11*, 119–134.38.

39. R. D. Hisrich & C. G. Brush. (1986). *The woman entrepreneur.* Lexington, MA: Lexington Books.

Chapter 2

The Women as College Students

In the previous chapter, we provided two frameworks, based on life stages and social changes, to describe and explain in general how women moved out of adolescence and into young adulthood in the 1970s, 1980s, and 1990s in the United States. Now we move to one specific group of women to illustrate these changes in greater detail.

HOW INFORMATION WAS GATHERED

In 1980–1982, 433 college junior and senior women participated in a study of their intentions to work for pay following childbirth. The students described their intentions, their beliefs about the consequences of working and not working, and their career and childrearing plans. They also answered questions about their family backgrounds and paid work experiences.

While in college, nearly three quarters of these women expected to have two or more future jobs, and half of them intended to work for pay during the first three years following childbirth. Although some women were less certain of their plans than others, women who would change their minds were not obvious.

Approximately a decade after they graduated, we located 335 participants from Phase I of the study for a follow-up mail questionnaire study focused on what they actually did in the intervening years and how their beliefs changed. Also, we conducted telephone interviews with about forty women to get more in-depth information about their employment and family experience in the decade between Phase I and Phase II. (Complete copies of the interview questions and mailed questionnaires are in Appendix A.) In Phase II we asked each woman about:

1. *Employment*—Her occupation, work history including company, industry, and promotions, as well as her reasons for leaving an organization after childbirth, her experience of sex discrimination or harassment in the workplace, and whether her job and salary expectations had been met. Also, we asked how she viewed the outcomes of working for pay on her career, her spouse, her child, and her financial well-being. We also asked her views about what employers could do to help women who wished to return to their jobs after childbirth.

2. *Family*—Her attitude toward and commitment to domestic life, her views about the role of a mother as exclusive caretaker, her actual child care arrangements and satisfaction with these arrangements, her fertility planning, and the level of her spouse's support for employment after childbirth. We also asked each woman what she saw as the consequences of not working for pay on her career, her spouse, her child, and her financial well-being.

3. *Biography*—Information about her parents, her education, her own and her spouse's income, her spouse's occupation, and the ages and number of her children.

We matched Phase I and Phase II questionnaires for 228 women (68 percent of those sent questionnaires and 52.6 percent of the original respondents). Responses from this group who answered our questions *both* in Phase I and Phase II form the basis of the following chapters.

FOUR GROUPS OF WOMEN

We classified women who responded to Phase II by how they acted on their college intentions. We divided women into four categories depending upon their intentions to return to paid work "within three years following the birth of their first child" as reported in Phase I and Phase II. See Table 2.1.

Careerists reported a higher probability that they would return to paid work rather than stay home in both Phase I and Phase II.

Homemakers reported a higher probability that they would stay home than return to paid work in both Phase I and Phase II.

Breadwinners reported a higher probability that they would stay home in Phase I and a higher probability that they would return to paid work in Phase II.

Nesters reported a higher probability that they would return to paid work in Phase I and a higher probability that they would stay home in Phase II.

Even though we were able to place almost all women in these four categories, in some cases women were still talking about future behavior in Phase II. Family life had been delayed longer than anticipated. In 1980, 91 percent expected to have had their first child by 1990. By 1990, only 46 percent had had at least one child. Of these, 20 percent had had two children and 4 percent had had three. The number of mothers and nonmothers in each group is described in Table 2.2.

Table 2.1
Groups of Women

Phase II

Intentions

		Work	Home
Phase I Intentions	Work	Careerists	Nesters
	Home	Breadwinners	Homemakers

Table 2.2
Distribution of Respondents by Group and Motherhood

Group	# of Mothers	# of Nonmothers	Total
Homemakers	27	20	47
Breadwinners	32	34	66
Nesters	5	10	15
Careerists	37	35	72
Total	110	99	209

Women who participated in both phases of the study live in urban and suburban Northeastern United States. They are predominantly Euro-American, one to three generations from immigration to the United States. As in other studies,[1] despite intensive efforts at recruitment, fewer African-American women responded to both questionnaires. As a result, the study does not represent their views as accurately, but we do retain the responses we have and comment on differences when they occur. Consistent with other studies of educated African-American women, their career behavior was more similar to that of educated white women than are careers of Afican-American and Euro-American women with less education.[2]

Women who responded to Phase II were less likely to be black, less likely to have lived in a large city, and less likely to have intended to return to work following childbirth than those who did not respond to Phase II (see Table 2.3). We attribute these differences primarily to lower availability of current addresses for one university which had more urban, black, career-oriented students than the other participating university.

Because we promised confidentiality to respondents, all names used in the book are fictitious and in a few cases, we combined responses of more than one person to protect women's individual identities and to report commonly stated ideas. When the same name is used in more than one place in the same chapter, we refer to the same woman.

COLLEGIATE PLANS

In Phase I, we identified the extent and nature of college women's plans. We asked them a series of questions about goals, strategies, possible blocks, and alternative plans for their careers. We asked similar questions about their plans for childrearing and their plans for combining their career and childrearing.

Because some people wonder whether women make plans, we wanted to answer the questions: Do women make plans for their future? If not, why not? If so, what are their plans like? What influences the extent to which they plan and the nature of their plans?

Defining a Plan

According to cognitive psychologists and artificial intelligence scholars,[3] a *plan* has a goal or a desired outcome and may contain one or more actions or strategies that could result in movement toward this goal. A *complex plan* could include smaller strategies for organizing several plans with each other, for choosing among alternatives, and for deciding when a plan should start and stop.

Table 2.3
Comparison of Phase I and Phase II Respondents

Race*	Phase I Only	Phase I and Phase II
Black	17%	6%
White	83%	94%
Religion		
Protestant	25%	21%
Catholic	40%	45%
Jewish	22%	18%
Other	12%	15%
Father's Education		
H.S. or less	53%	50%
Some college	13%	11%
College degree	22%	22%
Postgraduate ed.	11%	16%
Childhood residence*		
Rural	9%	8%
Town	53%	75%
Large city	38%	17%
1980 Intention to work*,a	.73	-.08

*Significant differences, Chi-square goodness of fit test, $p=.05$.
[a](probability she will work) – (probability she will not work) following childbirth: 1=very unlikely, 5=very likely.

A young woman's most sophisticated plans might include a future goal or image of what she wants for her paid work role as well as for her childrearing role. She might also have a variety of strategies for achieving each of these goals and a plan for combining them. She might have plans for combining her own plans with those of her partner, plans of alternatives she would try if she is blocked, and some notion of when the plans might begin and end. Less sophisticated planners might omit one or all of these components when they think about their future lives.[4]

Employment Career Plans

We define a career as a sequence of paid work experiences and attitudes extending through a person's work life.[5] According to a social psychological perspective, a career is the consequence of external role messages and internal preferences and talents. This perspective implies that women create plans for paid work as a result of their own self-knowledge and their interpretation of opportunities and constraints in their environment.

Out of 433 college women, only three had no career goal in mind when they were college students. Half of the black women and one-third of the white women reported very specific career goals, usually attainment of a particular occupation or profession.

Most women described strategies that involved only one step, and did not include obstacles or alternative plans. If they did anticipate problems, these were evenly divided among internal factors, such as lack of their own motivation or skill, and external factors, such as problems related to their husbands, their children, financial need, and lack of school or employment opportunities. If something blocked their first career plan they would try harder, change careers, or change jobs. Only 4 percent stated they might have a child if their initial career plans were blocked.

Thus, while most women had a general goal or direction, the majority had very limited career plans. Their plans involved few specific strategies and extended for only one or two years beyond college. Only about one-third of the black women and less than one quarter of the white women met the most sophisticated criteria for career planning—a specific goal, action strategies, and alternatives that extended far enough into the future to include more than one job or the attainment of a long-term goal in a single job (i.e., a career).

These descriptions of average career plans do not do justice to the variation in the extent of planning and the rich diversity of plans the women described. On one extreme, some women preferred to live life one day at a time and therefore, had few plans (about 15 percent). For example, Jane responded that she had no specific goals or strategies for her work, for her childrearing, or for combining the two. In the open-ended questions she reported:

I'd like to travel around—see the world and get myself into a good position in some kind of expanding, interesting career. Falling in love, getting married, and getting tied down in record time might prevent me from carrying out my plans. If that happens, my alternative is to live on a farm and raise and manage horses and children. If my answers are conflicting, it is because I really have no career in mind—even my education plans are indefinite, and my family plans are almost as sketchy.

The majority of women had some general plans but were vague on the details. For example, Mary had a goal of becoming an attorney. Her strategy was to "apply and be accepted by a law school and pass the bar once I've completed law school." The main block she saw was "not getting into law school right away or maybe not at all." Her alternative plans were to "work in an accounting firm or attend law school on a part-time basis."

Over one quarter of the women had very specific plans that extended ten or more years into the future. Clara said:

After I graduate from undergraduate school I plan to work in a CPA firm for about two years while going to grad school. During that time I will have gotten my CPA certificate. Working in the CPA firm will only be for the experience required by the state for CPA. After leaving the CPA firm, I plan to work for private industry. Falling in love and marrying earlier than I anticipated might prevent me from carrying out my plan. My alternative plans are vague, but I have considered opening my own clothing shop or trying to get a few modeling jobs, since I modeled part time while I was in high school.

About 10 percent of the women answered questions about their careers by discussing their family plans. Such a response indicated that the two plans were so intertwined in their minds that they merged into one.

Childrearing Plans

Childrearing plans comprise the unfolding sequence of childbirths and child care that women adopt based on their personal beliefs and preferences and their perceptions of the external realities. Most women believed they would have two or three children, two or three years apart, beginning when they were about age 27.

Plans for childrearing were less specific and extended further into the future than plans for a career or for childbearing. Many of these women's reports of childrearing strategies made clear how deeply the women were influenced by idealistic thinking in which their children, mostly male, would be perfect people living in a perfect home and world. Mary said:

I hope to raise my children in much the same way I was raised by my parents—to be independent, self-sufficient, and ambitious. Yet, I was also very secure and peaceful. I was taught to be very affectionate, loving, and to share what I had. I was given pride and self-confidence, and at the same time, I was taught humility and consideration for others. I will also give my children everything that is in my power to give them. My strategy is to spend as much time as possible sharing my life with my children, to teach them values and high morals, and to give them substantial religious background. I will mold them to be the kind of people I would want my husband and I [sic] to be. I will be patient with them without spoiling them in the extreme. If I married a man with whom I was unhappy, it might affect the way I would raise my children. I have no alternative plans if this plan is blocked.

Belinda reported:

I'd like to expose my child to all walks of life; to mingle, meet, live, and study with all types of people, different colors, religions, economic statuses. I would not want to influence but to encourage my child to do anything (as far as career is concerned) that he/she might endeavor. I would like to have some influence on my child's moral ethics (discipline/right and wrong).

The most obvious difference between career plans and childrearing plans was that childrearing plans sounded more like dreams than plans. Few considered strategies for coping with the financial burdens, the strains on a marital relationship, and the daily problems of diapers, sibling conflict, and childhood illnesses.

Plans for Combining Employment and Childrearing

Half of the white women and 84 percent of the black women expected to return to work within three years of the birth of their first children. Most of them had well-thought-out and specific plans for integrating their paid work and childrearing plans. The strategies for combining employment and childrearing most commonly included working part time, waiting until after the children were at school to return to work, hiring help in the home, placing their children in day care centers, or getting their husbands to help. The women anticipated common barriers to these strategies, equally divided between financial need and employer policies.

One young woman, who said she was more likely to work than not work during the first three years following the birth of her first child, planned to have three children, about two years apart, beginning when she was about 27 years old (four years into the future). Her career plans were to get an entry-level job in advertising, retailing, or wholesaling, and eventually work her way up into middle or top management. She expected to return to work anywhere from two months to one year after childbirth.

I plan to place the child in a child care center or have my husband take care of him if our work schedules allow it. This plan may be prevented by lack of adequate child care services or by having the same work schedules; then I would pay one of my sisters-in-law or one of our parents to watch the baby.

The accommodations that organizations might or might not make to women's efforts to combine a career with childrearing were ignored by some but considered very carefully by others. Clara, the woman whose specific career plans to be a CPA were described earlier, intended to have five children, beginning about six years in the future and spaced two years apart. Because of her career goals, she planned to have her first child later and have her children further apart than she might prefer. She stated that her childbearing plans had no effect on her career plans. Her strategy for combining her career and childrearing was as follows:

I don't plan on working long hours. I want to have a 9 to 5 job, basically, and when I come home from work, my time will be spent with my husband and children. If I have a job that requires a lot of overtime and a lot of travel, it would block this plan. (I can deal with a little overtime and a little travel.) I don't have any alternative plans yet if this plan is blocked, but if necessary, I will come up with one because I am going to have a career and a family, with children, no matter what (unless I am unable to have children).

Clara acknowledged the difficult life she might lead as an employee of a Big Six accounting firm early in her career and her willingness to postpone having children to gain this experience. However, once her childbearing began, she saw a very different kind of job for herself. We wondered where she would find such an accommodating job.

One student who felt the problem of combining a career and childrearing very strongly wrote a note on the back of her questionnaire:

This questionnaire finally made me seriously think about the choice between employment and childbirth. Although I view myself as *very* ambitious and career-oriented, I know that it will not be possible for me to balance climbing the corporate ladder and simultaneously caring for young children properly. The women who do this must be on speed. Hopefully, we will begin to see big corporations making more provisions for ambitious women with young children.

Another woman who planned to stay home and planned a childbearing pattern similar to those described above also, in some way, blamed corporations for her decision:

Although I plan to work when I have a child, I really don't think it should be as necessary as this society makes it. I believe it is important to have at least one parent available to the child, even if it becomes clear that adequate child care is available. My main gripe, however, is how the business world looks down at providing adequate facilities for working parents so that parents can work and be there for their child. I know that some companies have been able to incorporate this. I think all companies should. Not only would it be advantageous to the parent-child relationship, but it would provide a more fluid continuity of employees, especially female employees, and would give them the equal chance of furthering their careers without forsaking the privilege of raising a child.

Clearly, some women perceived problems in combining childrearing with careers in organizations that had little toleration for family life. Their responses displayed their frustration and anger as well as their willingness to alter childrearing plans in order to obtain the paid work they described. However, none of the women was sufficiently politicized to consider strategies that might influence organizations to change. Instead, all of them expected to be forced to change themselves. These perceptions among college students form the seeds of future job dissatisfaction and high turnover for organizations unwilling to address the needs of employees who are also parents.

In summary, less than one fourth of the college women met the optimal criteria for planning (that is, in response to leading questions, describing plans with multiple strategies and indicating consideration of possible obstacles and alternatives). Plans for combining a career and childrearing often were more specific than career or childrearing plans alone, but many plans of each kind express a dream-like wish for the ideal rather than a complete consideration of alternatives. This optimism is not unusual for reports of college women's plans in the 1970s. Thus, the responses in this study match the optimism reported in other women's plans or combining employment and homemaking.[6]

This lack of elaborate plans or strategies for achieving goals points to one reason why previous studies found little relationship between early career plans and later behavior. If women do not consider possible obstacles and do not make alternative plans for when they encounter such obstacles, they may be forced to abandon a goal and a plan altogether or be dissatisfied with the outcome.

COMPARISON BETWEEN PLANS AND REALITY

Despite the ambiguity and debate generated by social changes, college women did make choices about their future.[7] In some cases women followed early plans, in other cases, women's life experiences changed their intentions.

As the women in this study attempted to balance paid work, family, and personal needs, they often experienced feelings of anxiety or ambivalence.

Many wondered if they made the right choice or what might have happened if they had taken another path. In struggling to reduce the ambiguity with which they lived, some women gained a feeling of accomplishment that enhanced their sense of well-being.

In order to introduce each of the four groups—Careerists, Homemakers, Breadwinners, and Nesters—we have selected typical women to tell their stories. More complex descriptions and analyses are found in the following four chapters.

Careerists—An Employment Career

From their early years, Careerists tied their identity to hopes for a paid work career and continued a career immediately after childbirth. For these women, career opportunity coupled with boredom, and support for employment among friends, families, and co-workers, led them to reject a totally domestic lifestyle in favor of employment after childbirth.

One young woman, whom we call Cathy, is typical of this group. Cathy has consistently demonstrated strong enthusiasm for her career. Since graduating from college in the early 1980s, she has worked for an investment banking firm. Now an associate, she puts in 50-hour weeks. She always planned to continue her career after having a baby, although after childbirth she had some second thoughts and ambivalently reevaluated her return-to-work scenario. But, "In the end, the possibility of losing the chance for a promotion, as well as my skills and contacts, influenced me to return to work quickly. In addition, there were my own feelings of self-worth and accomplishment." Her life isn't easy, she says, but her husband shares the job of taking care of their son and running the household, and her employer occasionally allows her to work at home on her computer. What would it take for her to stay home with her child? "A change in my responsibilities with no further advancement potential, and even then I'd probably look for another job."

Homemakers—A Career in the Home

For other women, full-time domesticity provided a secure place and a healthy environment to raise children. For them a career in paid work had considerably less appeal. As far back as college, they believed that homemaking and domesticity would be a fulfilling experience and the one that best expressed their identity.

Even as a student, Helene said she wanted to stay home after the birth of her children. Now, nearly a decade later, she has carried out those plans.

She explains, "I always had a strong belief that children should be raised by their parents—and I still feel that way." Her beliefs are buttressed by traditional religious values that adhere to the view that mothers should stay home with their children if at all possible.

Like Cathy, Helene's decision to return to work after giving birth was made jointly with her husband. She said that "his job caused us to relocate frequently, so he wanted me to be at home with the children. As a result, I had a series of minor jobs, which were beneath my capabilities and not related to a career path. Most of my friends decided to stay home after their children were born, too, and this reinforced my decision." She said she felt satisfied with her life and had no burning desire to get back to paid work.

In college, Cathy and Helene each committed to a particular life-style tied to their identities. They imagined their futures in widely different terms, and their perceptions and experiences in the intervening years strengthened their initial views. Yet, many women who did not define themselves by either of these roles faced a more complex decision. In the interim between college and the births of their children, their experiences changed their expectations of what they could and could not accomplish. As a result, their priorities shifted and their plans changed. They acted in ways they had not foreseen.

Breadwinners–Unexpected Working Mothers

Although they preferred *not* to be employed after childbirth, some college women did not define themselves by either role. Later, the thought of full-time domesticity was no longer as attractive as it had seemed in college. These women responded to economic events in pragmatic, not ideological, ways by returning to paid work after childbirth. Beth, an accountant, explains:

In college I just assumed I'd stay home after the children were born. My mother stayed home with us, and I wanted my children to have that security. But after starting my career, I found that I really enjoyed working, and I wanted to advance my career. Also, we bought a house, and there was a big mortgage. Finally, my husband and I sat down and decided that if I could get someone really good to watch our child, I'd go back to work.

Now pregnant with her second child, Beth is currently employed. She says she plans to continue her employment career even after the birth of her second child.

Nesters—Unexpected Homemakers

Although intending to have careers in college, some women chose not to return to work after childbirth. For this group, life tragedies, poor employment experiences, and spouses who wanted them home, tended to push them out of the workplace. Nancy shed her work responsibilities when she felt she could not handle them and the additional demands of a baby.

At 30, I have had my first child. In deciding to stay home with my son, I considered attachment to my career versus bonding with the baby. [Another consideration is] the fact that my husband gets transferred periodically and the toll it has already taken on the progression of my career and attainment of higher level degrees. Also, during the past five years, I have observed and listened to many women—some who have remained home and others who have returned to work after childbirth. The sense of loss expressed by those who chose work was greater and more final over the long run than the full-time mothers.

Nancy has not returned to paid work during the years since the birth of her child. She said she does not have clear plans of when, or if, she will.

THROUGH THE LOOKING GLASS

In many ways, the women who came of age in the 1980s provide a looking glass for the next generation as they chart the future direction of their lives. Yet it is important to realize that because their lives have intersected with specific kinds of social change, women who came into the work force in the eighties have *created the change* as much as they have *been driven by it*. The convergence of multiple, and at times discordant, aspects of social change did not result in a uniform outcome of the career and family decisions of this group of women.

The Homemakers found mothering and homemaking to be the fulfilling experience they had hoped it would be; the Careerists found that paid work provided economic independence and room for personal growth and accomplishment, as the potential for upward mobility became more attractive than domestic life. Nesters were pushed out of the workplace by perceptions of reduced opportunities and family concerns, while Breadwinners were drawn in by expanding work opportunities and financial need.

In the following four chapters we take a closer look at how each group of women negotiated their postcollegiate decade, responding to their own plans and sense of self as well as to the changing world around them. Empirical data comparing college Phase I beliefs and young adult Phase II beliefs for each group are presented in each chapter. Data *comparing* groups are referred to in the narrative in the following four chapters and presented in tables in the Appendix. The concluding chapters summarize these comparisons and draw implications for women, their counselors, and their employers.

NOTES

1. L. Du Bois. (1984). Personal correspondence. United Negro College Fund.

2. E. L. Lehrer. (1992). The impact of children on married women's labor supply: Black-white differentials revisited. *The Journal of Human Resources, 27,* 421–444.

3. For example, see G. Miller, E. Galanter, & K. Pribram. (1960). *Plans and the structure of behavior.* New York: Holt, Rinehart and Winston.

4. For discussions and early studies of young women's plans and behavior, see S. Angrist & E. Almquist. (1975). *Careers and contingencies.* New York: Dunellen; H. S. Astin & T. Mynt. (1971). Career development of young women during the post-high school years. *Journal of Counseling Psychology, 18,* 369–393.

5. M. Arthur, D. Hall, & B. Lawrence. (1989). *Handbook of career theory.* New York: Cambridge University Press; see especially chapters 1, 6, 8, and 13 for discussions of special issues concerning women's careers in employment and family.

6. L. D. Cummings. (1977). Value stretch in definitions of career among college women: Horatia Alger as feminist model. *Social Problems, 25,* 65–74.

7. B. Gutek & L. Larwood. (1986). *Women's career development.* Newbury Park, CA: Sage.

Chapter 3

Careerists

Anne, a typical Careerist and a manager in a major pharmaceutical company, explains how she decided to return to work after her daughter was born:

Challenging projects to manage and good compensation for my time are important reasons to continue with my career after childbirth. Also, after three or four months, I think I'd get bored at home after adjusting to childbirth. I need variety in my life for happiness and I thrive on challenges. I also considered these factors in making my decision to go back to work: (1) adequate child care, (2) a four-days-a-week work schedule, and (3) finances.

My next-door neighbor is a close family friend and we hired her aunt to come to our house. Due to the nature of my position in my firm, I had to return ten weeks after the birth of our daughter. Because I have a very high-salaried job, I could afford to return on a less-than-full time basis, and still make a good salary. My husband and I agreed to this arrangement. Because of a long commute, he would be primarily responsible for child care on the days I work. He gets the baby sitter, takes her home and gets our daughter up and ready in the morning. In addition, my boss agreed to my schedule. I have been with him for eight years, so I was in a position to work around my needs, his needs and the baby's. If my boss hadn't agreed to my terms, then I would not have returned to work.

Both as students and young adults, Careerists planned to return to paid work soon after childbirth. This chapter explores three themes that promote this consistency: (1) their lifelong employment experiences, (2) their beliefs that employed mothers are doing what is best for themselves and their families, and (3) their positive evaluation of paid employment as identity affirming. Each section of this chapter examines one of these themes in greater detail to illustrate the dynamics of the Careerists' life patterns.

EMPLOYMENT CONCERNS

The women who remain committed to their careers from college through the first postgraduate decade believe that their paid work expresses a key part of who they are—their identities. As a result Careerists worked more than others before, during, and after college. In addition, they gained support from their own working mothers, their supervisors, and their own beliefs that employment would yield advancement, pride in achievement, income, and fun.

Preparation for Continuous Employment Careers

As college students, the Careerists enjoyed working and had more work experience than any other group: on average, about 30 hours a month compared to about 20 for the Homemakers (see Appendix, Table A.1). Even more telling, working mothers more often raised the Careerists, provided salient role models for combining employment and homemaking, and usually approved of their daughters' career-oriented choices (see Table 3.1). In fact, most of the Careerists' referents were more likely to approve of working mothers than the family and friends of Homemakers.

Table 3.1
Careerists' Perceptions of Approval of and Compliance with Referents

	Phase I		Phase II	
	Approval[d]	Compliance[e]	Approval[d]	Compliance[e]
1. Mother	3.49[a,b]	2.82[*]	3.53	2.44[*]
2. Father	3.24[a]	2.66	3.45	2.34
3. Husband	3.89[a,b]	3.99	4.12a[a]	3.94
4. Best Friend	4.03[a]	3.03	3.99	2.44
5. Boss	---	---	4.46[c]	2.26
6. Co-Worker	---	---	4.24[c]	2.12

*Phase I significantly different from Phase II
[a]Significantly different from Homemakers, $p > .05$
[b]Significantly different from Breadwinners, $p > .05$
[c]Significantly different from Nesters, $p > .05$
[d]1=very likely to disapprove, 5=very likely to approve
[e]1=I am unlikely to do as they wish, 5=I am likely to do as they wish

In some cases, mothers served as a positive role model that the daughters wished to emulate; in other cases, mothers taught their daughters what not to do. For example, Amy reported:

My mother worked for almost as long as I can remember and, if anything, I would say it had a positive influence upon me. Very rarely did I feel that I wasn't getting enough love or attention. I felt secure in my life and eventually grew to respect her being able to combine things so well. I only hope that I am able to combine both of these parts of my life as well as my mother has done.

Mothers who provided a pattern of how not to combine work and childrearing also elicited strong emotions and specific plans in their daughters. This pattern appeared to be more common in daughters of mothers who did not work. As one woman saw it:

My mother was home all the time during my and my brother's growing up and schooling. I came to rely on her too much. I'm not as independent as I would be if she had worked. I highly value personal growth, and I began to resent my mother's lack of growth. Therefore, I realize the importance of work. I am jealous of my friends whose mothers are entrepreneurs and career women.

Another young woman whose mother provided a positive role model reported her awareness of social class differences in maternal employment:

Mom worked part- then full-time by the time I was five. I'm healthy, well-adjusted, happy, and I love my parents. Mom worked it out. So can I, without bitching and moaning. My parents had very little money when they first got married. Poor people have had two incomes and have raised kids for decades. I feel that a lot of middle-class women who complain about working and raising kids are a product of pop psychology and sociology trends in this country. Why weren't the problems of working mothers studied before it became chic for middle-class women to work and raise children?

Relatively few college-educated women were working mothers when the women in our study were growing up in the 1960s and 1970s. Yet several studies carried out during this period reported that mothers who work—and enjoy working—are more likely to have career-oriented daughters who are more independent, more likely to view women as competent and have higher levels of self-esteem, findings consistent with the Careerists.[1]

The Careerists pursued advanced education after their undergraduate years, which also influenced their consistency between college plans and later experiences. Over 50 percent completed a graduate degree and about a quarter of this group obtained an LL.D., M.D. or Ph.D. This large investment in higher education also may explain why so many Careerists say they would feel guilty about not working after they had a child.

Working mothers, more education, and more personal work experience prepared the Careerists for a life of employment. Their experience on the job between college and childbirth reinforced these preferences.

Valuing Advancement, Income, and Fun

More than the Homemakers, the Careerists consistently value career achievement in the forms of advancement, maintaining job skills, and earning a good income (see Tables 3.2 and 4.2). Careerists think each of these is a source of pride and affirmation. Potential and opportunity, as much as actual work experiences, seem to play a part in keeping many Careerists in the work force. For example, more Careerists say they would leave a job with no opportunity for another job rather than becoming a homemaker (see Appendix, Table A.3).

Careerists take pride in the sense of mastery and competence they obtain from paid work. Ona, a systems analyst, says the main reason for her returning to work is to build on, or at least maintain, the career skills she has learned. She tells us that she feels good about her overall work contribution. "I returned to work quickly because no one covered my job adequately."

Enjoyment of work also motivates Careerists. Both as college students and as young adults, more Careerists than Homemakers see work as fun and fewer feel guilty about working (see Table 3.3).

Janice, a medical social worker, says she enjoys working and is not happy just being a mother at home. Also, she feels she might lose her career skills and she wants to work with other professionals.

The need to remain competitive in the labor market motivates women in several different occupations to return to work. Amy, a financial analyst, says one of her reasons for returning to work is to maintain job contacts and to keep abreast with her current skills. Carla, who works in publishing, says she returned to work as she always intended to because "I need to keep my mind sharp. I have a good career and I don't want to throw it away." In making the decision to return to work, she also considered the need to stay in touch with editorial contacts.

Along with valuing their career advancement, Careerists value themselves as economic providers. Says Luanne, an auditor, "Being independent and maintaining my earning potential are important to me because I saw my mother struggle financially after her divorce. Though I have a good marriage, financial dependence frightens me, so having my own income (it doesn't have to be very big) is very important to me." Amy, the financial analyst, tells us that even though maintaining her career skills is the major issue, she needs her income to feel secure about having a comfortable living.

Table 3.2
Values of Careerists

	Phase I	Phase II
Values[d]		
Having fun	4.37	4.38
A sense of accomplishment	4.68	4.69
Feeling tied down	1.68	1.77
Having variety in my life	4.09	4.03
Feeling guilty	1.25	1.34
Feeling resentful	1.23[*]	1.07[*]
Feeling tired	1.67	1.68
Feeling bored	1.49	1.40
Feeling close to my husband	4.85	4.85
Feeling close to my child	4.84	4.94
Running my household smoothly	3.84	3.90
Training my child myself	3.69	3.81[a]
Maintaining my career skills	4.41[a,*]	4.18[*]
Maintaining my job contacts	4.25[a,*]	4.00[a,*]
Advancing my career	4.21[a,*]	3.99[a,*]
Earning enough income myself	3.93[a]	3.86[a]
Having enough family income	4.56	4.55
Having extra income	4.05	4.12
Making more $ than it costs me to work	4.32	4.44
Husband needing two jobs	1.38	1.23
Missing child's growth milestones	1.69	1.55
Finding adequate child care	4.52[a,b]	4.69[a]
Having enough time for the child	4.57[a,*]	4.75[*]
Having enough time for myself	4.40	4.27

Table 3.2 (continued)

Values[d]	Phase I	Phase II
Having enough time for my husband	4.57	4.52
Husband helping around the house	4.48	4.44
Child will be independent	4.20	4.36
Child will be secure	4.67	4.78
Child will be well disciplined	4.44	4.56
Child will get along easily with others	4.53	4.68
Child will do better in school	----	4.42
Child will feel loved	4.88	4.90
Child will have attention when needed	4.55*	4.75*
Child feels closer to others than to me	2.16	2.07
Child will believe women are competent	----	4.66
Child will learn my beliefs	3.49	----

*Phase I significantly different from Phase II
[a]Significantly different from Homemakers, $p > .05$
[b]Significantly different from Breadwinners, $p > .05$
[c]Significantly different from Nesters, $p > .05$
[d]1=extremely undesirable, 5=extremely desirable

Supportive Supervisors and High Expectations

As students, Careerists had very high expectations of the world of work. As adults, they are not more likely to have their job expectations met, or to earn more money than the Homemakers, even though they might legitimately expect challenging, rewarding work in careers open to people with more advanced education (see Appendix, Table A.2).

Although they do not find the workplace better than they expected, the Careerists do have more support and approval from their bosses and their co-workers than women in the other groups (particularly Nesters). Given the day-to-day difficulties and occasional crises of managing work and family, a supportive work environment has made a major difference in their lives.

However, their bosses could not always change company policies, and several women commented on the lack of support for working mothers they found in other aspects of their work settings. Pat, an attorney, observes:

Table 3.3
Careerists' Perceptions of the Consequences of Working and Not Working Following Childbirth

	Phase I		Phase II	
Consequences[d]	Working	Not Working	Working	Not Working
Having fun	3.76[a]	3.42[b]	3.62[a]	3.61
A sense of accomplishment	4.41[a]	2.62[a,b]	4.11	3.01[a]
Feeling tied down	2.45	3.27[a]	3.16	3.47
Having variety in my life	3.99[*]	2.37[a,b*]	3.69[*]	2.65[a,*]
Feeling guilty	2.52[a]	2.56[a,b]	3.31[a]	2.50
Feeling resentful	1.84[b]	3.12[a,b]	2.66[a]	3.35[a]
Feeling tired	3.37	2.92	4.32	3.09
Feeling bored	1.84	3.58[a,b]	2.05	3.56[a]
Feeling close to my husband	4.03[*]	4.03[b]	3.68[*]	3.76[a]
Feeling close to my child	3.96[a,b]	4.41[a,*]	3.82	4.69[*]
Running my household smoothly	3.21	4.28	2.60	4.24
Training my child myself	3.15[*]	4.61	2.80[*]	4.67
Maintaining my career skills	4.37	2.51	4.22	2.03[c]
Maintaining my job contacts	4.35	2.37	4.26	1.96[c]
Advancing my career	4.20[*]	1.61	3.81[*]	1.51
Earning enough income myself	3.84	1.28	3.96	1.24
Having enough family income	4.36	2.99[a,*]	4.32	2.44[a,*]
Having extra income	3.97	2.21	3.88	1.53[a]
Making more $ than it costs				
me to work	4.00	1.41	4.08	1.48
Husband needing two jobs	1.40	2.76[a,b]	1.45	2.87[a]
Missing child's growth				
milestones	2.51	1.58	3.24	1.47
Finding adequate childcare	3.85	3.44	3.72[b]	2.94
Having enough time for the				
child	3.49[a]	4.69	3.10[b]	4.62
Having enough time for myself	3.00	4.14[*]	2.18	3.68[*]
Having enough time for my				
husband	3.51[a]	4.38[*]	2.64[a]	4.01[*]

Table 3.3 (Continued)

	Phase I		Phase II	
Consequences[d]	Working	Not Working	Working	Not Working
Husband helping around the				
house	4.43[*]	3.01[*]	3.89[*]	2.61[*]
Child will be independent	4.08	3.36	4.04	3.36
Child will be secure	4.01[a,b]	4.34	3.68[a]	4.27
Child will be well disciplined	3.96[a,b]	4.42[c]	3.64[a]	4.12[a]
Child will get along easily				
with others	4.23[a,b]	3.96	3.96[a]	3.72[a,b]
Child will do better in school	----	----	3.60[a]	3.81
Child will feel loved	4.43[a,*]	4.77	4.18[a,*]	4.67
Child will have attention when				
needed	4.85[a,*]	4.70	3.61[a,*]	4.71
Child feels closer to others				
than to me	2.91	2.23	2.78	1.96
Child will believe women are				
competent	----	----	4.07	3.81
Child will learn my beliefs	3.86	3.99	----	----

*Phase I significantly different from Phase II
[a]Significantly different from Homemakers, $p > .05$
[b]Significantly different from Breadwinners, $p > .05$
[c]Significantly different from Nesters, $p > .05$
[d]1=very unlikely, 5=very likely

I actually had considered taking some time off after my child was born, but I was concerned about losing seniority toward a partnership in my firm. I wish my organization would give longer maternity leave with part-time work first and full-time employment when I'm ready. But, there is an arrogant attitude toward pregnancy in my organization, that mothers need to be with their children. So they were not going out of their way to make adjustments for me when my daughter was born.

When asked what their employing organizations could do that would increase the likelihood of women returning to work after childbirth, most cite longer maternity leaves (at least six months) and more flexible hours, particularly starting times, because "mornings are hell."

Clearly the Careerists in our study—whether because of their mothers, their advanced education, their supportive supervisors, or their desire for a good income and personal achievement—think they can combine their work and family roles well. Part of this decision is contingent upon what they believe would happen at work if they stayed away too long, but the decision is also contingent upon what they believe would happen at home while they pursue their careers (see Table 3.3).

HOME CONCERNS

Careerists do not want to sacrifice their children and husbands in order to have the careers they desire. They have efficient time management, enough spouse support, and a dislike of homemaking to make it work.

The Strength of Time Management

Careerists consistently believe that they will have enough time to spend with their husbands and children. For Careerists, "enough time" means both time to interact with—and time to take care of—one's spouse and children (see Table 3.3).

Quite a few women say that working gives them *more* time for their relationships. Both as college students and young adults, more Careerists than Homemakers say that if they didn't work, their husbands would need to take extra jobs. Iris, an administrator at a pharmaceutical company, notes, "My husband and I decided that it was very important to our marriage to have some time together. We felt if I didn't return to work, he'd have to take a second job, and then we'd have little or no time together." Careerists believe that their paid work reduces the need for moonlighting, and thus contributes to the quality of their relationships.

Both in college and as young adults, Careerists also feel they will have enough time to feel close to, and care for, their children. They use many different strategies to achieve this goal. Some women report that much, if not most, of their free time is spent with their children. Others take some time via maternity leave—from six weeks to a year off. For others, switching to jobs with more flexible schedules or taking part-time jobs accommodates their needs.

Susan, a clinical social worker, meshes her desire to pursue her career with her need to be available for her child this way:

It is important for me to know that I would be available for my child as needed—during illness, special events, etc. I chose my employment schedule specifically with this in mind. Fortunately, I have a job that provides the stimulation I am looking for, enables me to begin training in my desired career, and affords me the schedule I need—three days a week. If I hadn't been able to find this arrangement along with adequate child care, I would not have gone back to work. Also, I did outline my schedule very carefully so that I was sure I would be available at certain times. When interviewing, I already knew a flexible schedule was important and discussed this then. It was important to get the schedule I needed, three days a week.

Accommodating their schedules to their husband's and children's needs, while not ignoring their own needs, enables the Careerists to carry out their college plans.

Supportive Spouses

Give-and-take relationships with their spouses encourage Careerists' personal aspirations. This support includes providing an egalitarian relationship, emotional support, practical help, and sharing the financial burdens of the family.

As college students, Careerists expected their future husbands to play a significant role in their plans for combining a career and childrearing. A future personnel training specialist planning two children, four years apart, beginning when she was 28 to 30, stated:

Ideally, I would hope that I am fortunate enough to marry a man who will equally share childrearing responsibilities. By this I mean that he will spend as much time with the children as I do, including taking time off from work and interrupting his career.

This woman at least acknowledged that this was an ideal that might not be achieved. More commonly, plans for future husbands described an unlikely perfection. For example, Claire, who wanted to travel and was seeking a job in the airlines industry, planned one to two children beginning when she was about age 27, and intended to return to work within six months to a year after childbirth. This career and childbearing plan depended heavily upon marrying the right husband. In college she was living with a future accountant:

My husband and I will have good paying jobs, hopefully, to give my family many things needed and wanted. We will work the same hours, so when we see our child, it will be together. I will find a good day care service. I now work for a day care center, and I can pretty well judge a good one from a bad one. And the rest of the care will be from my husband and myself. It's the *quality* of time spent, not *quantity*, [that matters].

If I work for the airlines, I may have unusual hours, but seniority may improve that. Or the work may take me on trips where I may not see my husband or child for a week or so. I don't think this would be detrimental to my relationship with them, though. My husband can be just as caring and loving as I can be to our own child. If I do have to leave for a while, my child will be well taken care of.

Often there was an overtone of a normative requirement—a husband "should" do these things—rather than a careful consideration of what women believed would most likely happen. Because of these desires, the Careerists may have had or sought mates with less traditional expectations of their wives. Also, over time, their relationships may have evolved in a way that was qualitatively different from the Homemakers' relationships (see Table 3.1 and Table 4.1). This also may have been reinforced by the changing social norms that now facilitate more egalitarian marital relationships.

As adults, the Careerists think that employment enhances their relationships with their spouses by making themselves more equal and more desirable companions. Many women talk about how the decision to return to work was made jointly with their husbands. Said Carolyn, an auditor with the federal government: "I have always known that I would return to work—my husband and I both discussed it, and we agreed. We feel it makes me a more interesting person."

Many women believe their husbands provide a great deal of emotional support and encouragement for their careers, both before and *after* parenthood. But the Careerists expect more than emotional career support. They want practical help as well. Anecdotal evidence indicates greater sharing of household and child care responsibilities among this group.

Despite this optimistic attitude, reality altered the Careerists' perceptions, however. The Careerists believe their husbands will help with the housework—yet, they were significantly more likely to believe this as college students than later (see Table 3.3). As with many dual-earner couples of this generation, while men with working wives spend somewhat more time on child care and family chores than in the past, they usually do not do as much as their wives.

Working also facilitates relationships with Careerists' spouses, because it reduces the financial burden husbands otherwise would have to shoulder. According to Joanne, a computer programmer:

We need the money so that my husband does not have to have two jobs. We had to find someone to watch our son. Fortunately, we had our parents there to help. If we did not have them, I probably would have settled for part-time work at night. My husband and I periodically talked about my going back to work when we first got married. He always wanted me to go back to work after our child was born, because it would be a lot of pressure for him to be the only money-maker in the family.

Family income and extra income would shrink if the Careerists were not employed; yet, much of this issue deals with perception of need. The husbands of the Careerists do not earn any less than the husbands of the Homemakers (see Appendix, Table A.1). Yet, fewer Careerists than Home-makers believe they would have enough family income if they do not work outside the home. Also, more Careerists than Homemakers think their husbands would need an extra job if they do not work (see Table 3.3 and Table 4.3).

Disdain for Domesticity

On the whole, Careerists do not enjoy the thought of domesticity. As college students, Careerists more than Homemakers and Breadwinners thought that by not working, they would have less variety and accomplish-ment in their lives and would feel more guilty, bored, and resentful. A decade later, the Careerists still perceive negative consequences from not working outside the home, and they are even less likely to believe they would have enough time for themselves if they are unemployed.

Many Careerists find the homemaker role, in particular, unattractive. Researchers have concluded that while virtually all women enjoy being mothers, they do not necessarily enjoy housekeeping.[2] For some women, being home on a full-time basis can be more tiring than combining paid work and family.

Talia, a fashion illustrator, tells us that she would miss and need work, people, and an office environment if she did not return to work after her child was born. "I need other interests—not just those at home. I am not 'Suzy Homemaker,'" she says.

We asked women who were mothers the extent to which they agreed or disagreed with statements such as "I am willing to put in a great deal of effort beyond that normally expected to be successful as a homemaker" and "Often, I find it difficult to agree with the values espoused by homemakers" (see the Phase II questionnaire Appendix A, "Commitment to the Home-maker Role"). Of the four groups of women in our study, Careerists have the lowest total scores on this part of the questionnaire, and are significantly less likely than Homemakers to feel committed to their role as a homemaker (see Appendix, Table A.4).

The limited commitment to the homemaker role enables the Careerists to manage their family role without much guilt or conflict. Giving this role low priority creates less conflict with their work role. That is, if they really enjoyed homemaking, or thought they should be engaged in tasks at home when they were working, the opportunity for work-family conflict would increase.

CHILD CONCERNS

In contrast to each of the other groups, the Careerists—both in college and as adults—firmly believe that their working outside the home will have a positive impact on their children (see Table 3.3; compare to Tables 4.3, 5.3, and 6.3). This belief consists of three components: first, children can be quite young when a mother returns to work; second, children's socioemotional needs can be served better if mothers are working; third, adequate child care arrangements are beneficial to their children.

When Should Mothers Return to Work?

As young adults, Careerists expected to return to work full time when their children were slightly more than a year old, whereas Homemakers, Breadwinners, and Nesters believed the child should be seven, six, and five, respectively. As young mothers, Careerists continue to believe they should return to work when the child is quite young. For example, one woman who cites "good child care and a convenient work site" as reasons for returning to work shortly after her child was born said:

Five to six months is the age for mothers to start working full time. Any earlier is too much stress for the mother. At this stage, the child is usually on a schedule and the mother has the opportunity to bond with the child and provide adequate breast feeding, if desired.

Occasionally, experience changes their views. Jane, an assistant buyer for a large retailer, reports:

With child number one, I went back to work six weeks after giving birth in order to maintain my position. There was no family leave policy. Financially, I also needed to work. Adequate day care was important. I was able to work part-time hours for the first six months after birth. With child number two, I was able to stay home for one year prior to returning full time. By then, I needed to go back to work for my sanity.

When asked what she believes, realistically, is the best child's age for a mother to start working full time, Jane replies:

I think one year. I went back after six weeks and after one year. I think the year was wonderful! I felt rested, bonded with my son, and ready to go back. With my daughter, I was not really ready to return after six weeks.

In sum, Careerists attempt to harmonize their own and their children's needs in their decisions about when to return to work.

Costs and Benefits to the Child

Careerists link the attitude that a mother can return to work when her child is quite young with beliefs that working is beneficial to children's growth and development. For example, as college students, more Careerists than Homemakers and Breadwinners believed that if they worked after childbirth, their children would be secure, disciplined, and sociable, would feel loved, and would get enough attention. A decade later, more Careerists than Homemakers hold substantially the same views. They also believe their children will do well in school (see Table 3.3; compare to Tables 4.3, 5.3, and 6.3). They are somewhat more pessimistic now than they were as college students that their children will feel loved and get enough attention if they are working, but they are still more optimistic about this than Homemakers are.

Some Careerists even believe that staying home would have a *negative* impact on their children's socioemotional development. For instance, as college students, the four groups of women did not differ in their beliefs about the impact on the child if they stayed home. Now, more Careerists believe that if they stay home their children will be *less* sociable than if they work. However, they are slightly more likely as adults than they were as students to believe they would feel closer to their children if they were *not* working, and less likely to train their children themselves if they are working.

A substantial number of Careerists justify the timing of their return based on their knowledge of children's development. According to one, "By that age [6 months], the child is more independent and does not need as much attention as a newborn." Some mothers seemed influenced by what they remembered from their child psychology courses. Jeanne, now an attorney, believes six to nine months is an appropriate age to return, because "it allows time for bonding, but before separation anxiety set in." In terms of a child's sociability, most women seem to feel that children benefit if mothers return to work when children are age two, because, by this age, "a child should learn to reach out." According to one mother, "A two-year-old child is no longer a baby and can be more independent and socialize with other children."

Others point to the importance of the health and disposition of their children. Frances, a radiologist, observes:

I wanted to be there for the first year, so I could get to know my child and give her the love and attention she needed. But another reason that I waited was that she was always getting sick and I didn't want to call up sick half the time.

Another noted, "It is easier to return to work with a 'good' baby than a 'bad' baby." Michelle, a manager in a state agency, tells us, "My child was independent from the beginning. He was also very even-tempered and loved being with other people, which made everything easier."

Child Care Arrangements

Availability of good child care determines when many women return to paid employment. In contrast to Breadwinners and Homemakers, Careerists were concerned about and valued finding good child care when they were college students. They believed they could find good care. This belief persists today and seems to reduce guilt about returning to work soon after childbirth (see Tables 3.2 and 3.3). For instance, Jean, a nurse, says:

I am very familiar with day care centers. This is because I had one myself for a while, and worked in one during college. I have faith in many day care providers. Therefore, I will feel no guilt. And I am a firm believer in quality time, not quantity time.

Availability of child care also influences whether Careerists work full time or part time. Jennifer, a middle school teacher, explains: "I knew from the beginning that I would stay home with my newborn son for the first year. I don't believe I could have found adequate child care for my son while he was still an infant. A full day at a day care is very tiring for a young child."

Judy, a manager in major telecommunications organization who has not yet had a child, discusses her plans:

I don't want to go back to work too quickly—about six months after birth would be fine. Primary consideration in returning to work will be the availability of quality day care. If it is not available, I may only work part time. If it is, I'll be free to concentrate on work during the work day.

Many other women in the Careerist group say child care has never been a major problem because they are willing to use a variety of types of care. Some have live-in help or nannies. Luanne, the auditor, says that because she has a relationship with a live-in sitter that satisfies her, she felt comfortable returning to work when her son was only three months old. Quite a few use friends or relatives to baby sit. One woman's sister-in-law lives nearby and is very dependable. Another says both sets of grandparents alternate in taking care of her two-year-old daughter, and a third Careerist says a good friend owns a preschool and her daughter stays there. Alternatively, a third-grade teacher has temporarily taken a job as a nursery school teacher in order to be near her son.

Other women schedule back-up arrangements in the event something happens to their primary child care arrangement. Maria, a financial analyst, whose baby stopped nursing at three months and who returned to work when the baby was seven months old told us:

A family friend is baby sitting while I work. I have confidence in her. She also has children of her own for our son to play with. Also, my company opened a new day care center and I can use it on a drop-in basis as needed.

While most of the attention on child care focused on early childhood, among women with older children, difficulties in getting children to outside activities and making arrangements to pick up and drop off children during school hours caused the most headaches.

In summary, the Careerists are optimists when it comes to their children. They are reasonably confident that their children will not be harmed; in fact, they think their children benefit from early exposure to other children and adults. They are also confident that good child care is available and are innovative and thorough in making initial and back up plans to assure their children are well cared for.

SELF CONCERNS

Much of the Careerists' positive self-concept and feelings of competence comes from clear priorities and identification with the salience of the work role. Their positive feelings about work, their resentment at the thought of being a full-time homemaker, and their conviction that their preference will not harm their families reinforce this choice.

Pride in Accomplishment

The responses to the questionnaire that asked about feelings of competence and self-confidence in Phase II (see Appendix in Table A.5) reveal pride in the way the women have managed their lives. For many, paid work is a key to their identity. Lisa, now pregnant with her first child, expresses this clearly:

Although becoming a mother is very important to me, becoming a housewife is not the "end-all, be-all" of aspirations! I plan to work at least part time to continue to be the individual that I am. I don't want to be just "so and so's Mom."

As Pat, an administrator for an engineering firm, explains,

I feel that I would be a much better mother if I combined motherhood with employment. I think I would be more fulfilled and feel a sense of accomplishment about my life.

Careerists not only value work, they find the alternatives considerably less appealing and gain self-esteem from acting according to their priorities. Although many Careerists have been willing to change jobs or reduce their hours to accommodate their children's needs, they do not enjoy domesticity. Brenda, a customer service manager in a large bank, with a two-year-old daughter, puts it this way:

When I considered becoming a mother, I firmly felt I would return to work in the months following childbirth. I wanted to return to the position I held. I did not want to stay home because (1) I took a long time to decide and establish a career path that I did not want to relinquish quickly, and (2) raising a child requires more energy and discipline than I have. It has many boring hours between the exciting moments. I have a hard time enjoying the excitement after spending a lot of time being bored.

As much as they love their children, many Careerists do not see full-time domesticity as a rewarding way of life and are satisfied because they have been able to arrange their lives to suit their values.

CONCLUSION

In the midst of an ambiguous environment, the Careerists have selected people and experiences that support their identity-affirming choices to become employed mothers. Childhood experiences such as having an employed mother, adolescent experiences such as working for pay more as college students, and adult experiences such as having a supportive employer and spouse contribute to their employment consistency. In addition, the Careerists' beliefs include several consistent themes. First, they want to maintain their career accomplishments and earn an income, as well as have a family. Second, they believe they can manage their time well enough to do both, with a supportive spouse willing to share family responsibilities. Third, they believe the benefits their children receive by their working far outweigh any costs, as long as they obtain adequate child care. Finally, since much of their identity derives from their work role, they enhance their self-esteem by setting clear priorities that enable them to spend more time doing what they like to do (i.e., working for pay) and less time doing what they don't like to do (i.e., homemaking).

Overall, they are happy with their choices, and happy with their lives. However, compared to themselves as college students, their careers have become somewhat less important to them over time (see Table 3.2). This change may be due to several different processes occurring simultaneously. First, individual differences exist within this group. For instance, some women value their careers more than others. Second, changing cultural norms support women postponing childrearing while establishing their careers. Such social support may lessen the need to be adamant when answering questionnaires about career orientation. Third, some women slow their careers when they have young children.

Psychologists concerned with changes in adult development suggest that women who emphasize building careers in their twenties often are interested in building families in their thirties and vice versa.[3] Even though they have returned to work virtually full time, some women have placed their career advancement on temporary hold following childbirth. Most continue working full time in order not to go backward—to stop working is to risk losing valuable networks—but some do not expect to advance. Quite a few have moderately reduced their hours, found flexible hours, work at home, or are on a part-time schedule for a short while after maternity leave. Others temporarily have taken jobs that are less pressured and more compatible with family needs. When asked about their career planning after they have had their babies, many Careerists reply that they are "taking things one day at a time."

In addition to explaining this change by looking at lifespan development, we can look at the external circumstances of Careerists' lives. How Careerists view their careers interacts with how their organizations view the Careerists. For example, as college students, the Careerists were more likely to consider variety and career advancement as outcomes of working than they were as adults. Thus, a decade into their careers, they are more likely than the Homemakers to see advancement as desirable, but no more likely than women in the other three groups to see it as a likely outcome of working (see Tables 3.3, 4.3, 5.3, and 6.3). Careerists want their organizations to do more for career women, particularly with regard to better promotion opportunities, longer childbirth leave, on-site day care, and flexible hours. Careerists are running into the glass ceiling reported by many in the U.S. Department of Labor (USDL) studies of this phenomenon[4] and are requesting the same assistance identified in the more recent USDL study of working women.[5]

If we look at ambivalence, as a group, the Careerists seem remarkably free of anxiety, in spite of juggling multiple roles and complex time schedules. They also seem consistently motivated by a need for achievement and are satisfied with the ways in which they have sought to fulfill these needs.

The primary unresolved ambivalence in their lives arises from the question of whether they are constructing their particular paid work-family pattern for the benefit of themselves, their spouses, their children, or some combination thereof. Individuals vary in their justification. Some clearly make a self-enhancing choice, others more easily justify a rapid return to employment by claiming that it is better for their husbands not to have to work two jobs and for their children to develop socially.

Their lives are not completely without ambiguity, however. The primary ambiguity seems to revolve around acceptance and support of their choices by employers and organizational policies. Careerists express a wistfulness, occasionally tinged with anger, that they would like to be able to get more institutional support for combining two roles for at least the first or second year after childbirth. But they believe the current nature of corporate careers makes this a very costly wish—and one they are willing to give up, especially if the alternative is to adopt what they see as a "boring Suzy Homemaker role." Organizational responses to Careerists making elaborate plans to return to work earlier than they would personally prefer exaggerate their ambivalence. Careerists believe their employers not only do not acknowledge their dedication, but also might punish them by denying advancement because of a glass ceiling or because some in the organization think they really belong at home. Such suspicions have been empirically supported by findings that being a mother is negatively related to receiving coaching, and spending time on household activities detracts from receiving coaching, key assignments, and increased job responsibilities.[6]

In spite of some lingering ambiguity and ambivalence regarding how organizations perceive their choices, Careerists maintain their self-confidence and life satisfaction by adhering to their central beliefs: They have fashioned lives for themselves that are internally consistent and supported by those closest to them.

NOTES

1. S. J. Vodanovich & T. J. Kramer. (1989). An examination of the work values of parents and their children. *The Career Development Quarterly, 37*, 365–374.

2. F. J. Crosby (Ed.). (1987). *Spouse, parent, worker.* New Haven, CT: Yale University Press.

3. S. Ornstein & L. Isabella. (1990). Age vs. stage models of career attitudes of women: A partial replication and extension. *Journal of Vocational Behavior, 36*, 1–19.

4. U.S. Department of Labor. (1991). *A report on the glass ceiling initiative.* Washington, DC: U.S. Department of Labor, Lynn Martin, Secretary.

5. U.S. Department of Labor. (1994). *Working women count: A report to the nation.* Washington, DC: U.S. Department of Labor, Women's Bureau, Karen Nussbaum, Director.

6. S. D. Friedman, J. H. Greenhaus, & S. Parasuraman. (1994). *The impact of family structure on career development opportunities.* Paper presented at the Academy of Management Meeting, Dallas, TX.

Chapter 4

Homemakers

Hannah, a woman who has chosen to leave her paid work after childbirth, explains her choice this way:

I feel it is very important for me to be home for my child. At this time, we are able to afford for me not to work, and this made my decision much easier. My mother was home with us, and I always found comfort knowing that she was there. I want my child to feel that same security. I spoke to other women who needed to return to work, and they expressed a desire to be home with their children. Therefore, I feel fortunate to be able to be home.

Also I have a desire to see the household and family run as smoothly as possible. Of course, our financial situation is important, but it is not the primary consideration. Maintaining my career skills is last on my list.

If one were to ask the Homemakers why they chose not to return to work, they would most likely reply that they do work. They work "raising children— the most important work a woman can do." While all groups want to do a good job raising their children, Homemakers take pride in holding this conviction as central to their identities. Their pride in creating a home centered on important family values contributes to their overall sense of well-being even though they now live a life-style that is less common than that of mothers who work outside the home. They overcome the potential anxiety of not conforming to the prevalent social trends of employed mothers by surrounding themselves with family and friends who believe as they do (see Table 4.1).

Table 4.1
Homemakers' Perceptions of Approval of and Compliance with Referents

	Phase I		Phase II	
	Approval[d]	Compliance[e]	Approval[d]	Compliance[e]
1. Mother	2.49[a]	3.0	2.91	2.85
2. Father	2.38[a]	2.94	2.84	2.80
3. Husband	2.72[a,c]	3.83	3.04[a,b]	3.73
4. Best Friend	3.25[a]	2.77	3.62	2.20
5. Boss	---	---	4.16[d]	1.98
6. Co-worker	---	---	4.00[d]	1.96

[a]Significantly different from Careerists, p > .05
[b]Significantly different from Breadwinners, p > .05
[c]Significantly different from Nesters, p > .05
[d]1=very likely to disapprove, 5=very likely to approve
[e]1=I am unlikely to do as they wish, 5=I am likely to do as they wish

In most ways, Homemakers hold attitudes and values that are exactly opposite those of the Careerists. Homemakers parallel Careerists in the consistency and centrality of the beliefs and values that anchor their identities and, therefore, their life patterns over time. In this consistency, certain themes stand out. Homemakers raise their children as their "real work." While all groups want their children to thrive, Homemakers believe no one can do this job as well as a mother. They adhere to this belief because they feel they are good at what they do and enjoy a domestic rather than a paid-work life-style. Their spouses share this view and generally support the traditional division of labor, where wives run the household and husbands earn the income. Finally, they accept their husband's income as adequate and are willing to forgo their own income in order to maintain this life-style.

HOME CONCERNS

Family-Centered Lifestyles

Homemakers have clear priorities. Even as college students, the pleasure of raising their children clearly outweighs any other career plans. Since their attachment to a homemaking career is central to their identities, they filter out contradictory social messages and pay close attention to those facts and people that support their family-centered views.

Homemakers believe three things characterize their family-centered values and priorities (see Table 4.2). First, both as college students and as adults they fully enjoy domesticity and believe they should remain as child caretakers in the home rather than maintaining their employment skills and job contacts. Second, they have a partnership with their spouses based upon traditional sex role values where husbands, rather than wives, provide income. And third, to carry out these wishes, they willingly forgo the additional income they would earn. Their values changed little in the decade between Phase I and Phase II.

Fewer Homemakers' mothers worked outside the home when Homemakers were young, and Homemakers' mothers who chose to stay home also served as a source of schemata about how to make this decision (see Appendix, Table A.1). A young college woman who believed it was less likely she would work after childbirth reported:

I have a wonderful mother who devoted 25 years of her life to her children. We have a close and important relationship. I hope someday I can be as good a mother as she was. The question is, does it take 25 years of devotion? I realize how important it was for me to have her home when I needed her.

As college students, their friends and family were much less likely than Careerists to approve of working mothers. A decade later, their husbands also are less likely than husbands of women who are employed to approve of their wives working (see Table 4.1).

Attachment to Domesticity

Compared to Careerists, more Homemakers believe the homemaker role has greater variety and accomplishment. And, both as college students and as adults, fewer Homemakers say they would feel bored, tied down, or resentful about staying home with their children (see Table 4.3). They enjoy the domestic arts and feel mothers should stay home because otherwise they would not have enough time for their families or for themselves. As adults, Homemakers believe more than Breadwinners and Nesters that they would not have enough time for themselves if they work outside the home. They also are less sure as adults than they were as college students that they would have enough time for themselves if they stay at home after childbirth. Yet, overall, these women speak little about their own activities and leisure. They care more about not having enough time for their husbands and children if they engage in paid work. Several women equate time for themselves with the time they would have spent on a career rather than the time they deserve

Table 4.2
Values of Homemakers

Values[d]	Phase I	Phase II
Having fun	4.07[*]	4.40[*]
A sense of accomplishment	4.46	4.62
Feeling tied down	1.89	1.85
Having variety in my life	3.76	3.93
Feeling guilty	1.16	1.14
Feeling resentful	1.09	1.14
Feeling tired	1.59	1.51
Feeling bored	1.44	1.46
Feeling close to my husband	4.89	4.80
Feeling close to my child	4.91	4.87
Running my household smoothly	4.14	4.06
Training my child myself	4.11	4.44[a,b]
Maintaining my career skills	4.04[a]	3.80
Maintaining my job contacts	3.74[a]	3.20[a,b]
Advancing my career	3.58[a]	3.38[a]
Earning enough income myself	3.20[a,b,c]	3.40[a]
Having enough family income	4.42	4.53
Having extra income	3.78	4.00
Making more $ than it costs me to work	3.94	4.06
Husband needing two jobs	1.47	1.31
Missing child's growth milestones	1.47	1.29
Finding adequate child care	3.91[a,b]	3.98[a,b]
Having enough time for the child	4.82[a,*]	4.78[*]
Having enough time for myself	4.27	4.33
Having enough time for my husband	4.71	4.58

Table 4.2 (Continued)

	Phase I	Phase II
Values[d]		
Husband helping around the house	4.22	4.14
Child will be independent	4.11	4.27
Child will be secure	4.80	4.78
Child will be well disciplined	4.46	4.60
Child will get along easily with others	4.67	4.62
Child will do better in school	---	4.46
Child will feel loved	4.94	4.94
Child will have attention when needed	4.85	4.74
Child feels closer to others than to me	2.07	1.84
Child will believe women are competent	---	4.56
Child will learn beliefs	3.59	---

*Phase I significantly different from Phase II
[a]Significantly different from Careerists, p > .05
[b]Significantly different from Breadwinners, p > .05
[c]Significantly different from Nesters, p > .05
[d]1=extremely undesirable, 5=extremely desirable

for leisure. They believe that time for themselves can wait until they no longer have children at home.

Spouse-Valued Homemakers

Homemakers define their relationships with their spouses based upon a synchrony of values and belief in maintaining traditional sex roles. The couple's shared values define an important component of their marriages just as common values define the Careerists' more egalitarian marriages.

In many cases, husbands have a negative attitude toward their wives' employment. Such attitudes combined with the Homemakers' weak interest in paid work reinforce their desire not to return to paid work after childbirth. Jackie attributes her decision to stay home to "my husband's commitment to the ideal that the mother should be at home with the child, as well as my own desire to be at home and my husband's ability to support the family." Belinda expresses similar thoughts:

Table 4.3
Homemakers' Perceptions of the Consequences of Working and Not Working Following Childbirth

Consequences[d]	Phase I		Phase II	
	Working	Not Working	Working	Not Working
Having fun	3.27[a]	3.73	2.98[a,b,*]	4.02
A sense of accomplishment	3.74[a]	3.57[a,c]	3.78	3.80[a,*]
Feeling tied down	2.71	2.65[a,*]	3.30	3.24[*]
Having variety in my life	3.74	2.98[a]	3.51	3.24[a,b]
Feeling guilty	3.14[a]	1.74[a,c]	4.14[a,b]	1.98
Feeling resentful	2.24	2.07[a,c]	3.40[a]	2.22[a,b]
Feeling tired	3.44[*]	2.46[c,*]	4.34[*]	3.00[*]
Feeling bored	1.80[*]	2.60[a,c]	2.27[*]	2.78[a]
Feeling close to my husband	3.72[*]	4.30	3.27[b,*]	4.34[a]
Feeling close to my child	3.33[a]	4.56	3.26[a,b]	4.78
Running my household smoothly	3.02	4.34	2.40	4.36
Training my child myself	2.73[c,*]	4.53	2.32[b,*]	4.73
Maintaining my career skills	4.26	2.73	4.34	2.44
Maintaining my job contacts	4.18	2.54[*]	4.38	2.13[*]
Advancing my career	4.22	2.00	4.07	1.58
Earning enough income myself	3.82	1.56	3.84	1.44
Having enough family income	4.39	3.44[a]	4.36	3.60[a,b]
Having extra income	3.98	2.67	4.26	2.54[a,c]
Making more $ than it costs				
me to work	3.96	1.78	4.11	1.62
Husband needing two jobs	1.31	2.09[a]	1.42	2.07[a,b]
Missing child's growth milestones	3.42[a]	1.67	3.84[b]	1.42
Finding adequate child care	3.40	2.94	3.16[a,b]	2.63
Having enough time for the child	2.87[a,c]	4.66	2.16[a,b]	4.73
Having enough time for myself	2.76	4.26[*]	1.74[c,b]	3.80[*]

Table 4.3 (Continued)

	Phase I		Phase II	
Consequences[d]	Working	Not Working	Working	Not Working
Having enough time for my husband	2.91[a,c]	4.49	2.04[a,b]	4.22
Husband helping around the house	4.18*	3.28	2.76*	2.94
Child will be independent	3.83	3.43	3.67	3.73
Child will be secure	3.22[a]	4.33*	2.91[a,b]	4.58*
Child will be well disciplined	3.46[a,c]	4.20*	3.04[a,b]	4.46[a,*]
Child will get along easily				
with others	4.67[a]	3.89*	3.47[a,c]	4.18[a,*]
Child will learn my beliefs	3.59	3.96	---	---
Child will feel loved	4.94*	4.73	3.62[a,b]	4.82
Child will have attention when needed	3.96[a,b]	4.76	2.96[a,b,*]	4.72
Child feels closer to others				
than to me	2.07	2.18	3.26	2.11
Child will believe women				
are competent	---	---	3.76	4.04
Child will do better in school	---	---	3.02[a,c]	4.15

*Phase I significantly different from Phase II
[a]Significantly different from Careerists, $p > .05$
[b]Significantly different from Breadwinners, $p > .05$
[c]Significantly different from Nesters, $p > .05$
[d]1=very unlikely, 5=very likely

My husband earns enough to support a family comfortably. We have everything we need and some of the things we want. I do not particularly enjoy working—I was doing it to earn money, not because I had a career goal in mind. My husband did not want me to work, so all things considered, staying home was an easy decision to make.

Consistent with these couples' value synchrony, Homemakers find being emotionally available for their families rewarding. As adults, Homemakers believe they will feel closer to their husbands if they are not working, and as adults they are even more convinced than they were in college that they would *not* feel close to their husbands if they are employed. They invest heavily in maintaining close ties, a pattern consistent with a traditional female gender role sense of "connectedness."

The traditional division of labor implies that their spouses expect them to perform most domestic tasks. In turn, fewer Homemakers expect their spouses to share running the household. As college students, Homemakers expected their spouses to help if they were employed mothers, but as adults, they expect little help whether they were or were not employed. As part of this division of labor, Homemakers also make do with less money rather than putting financial pressure on their husbands to work two jobs to compensate for their wives' lack of paid work.

Make-Do Family Finances

Money clearly does not motivate Homemakers. Thus they differed from the Careerists by continuing to believe that even if they do not work, they will have enough family income. Also, unlike the Careerists, Homemakers do not think their husbands would need to take an extra job or moonlight to make ends meet because they themselves are not employed (see Table 4.3).

Interestingly, although the spouses of Homemakers do not earn significantly more than the spouses of Careerists, Homemakers believe their family income is sufficient (see Appendix, Table A.1, Table 4.3, and Table 3.3). Elise, an accountant who does not yet have children, says:

Hopefully, I will be able to stay home until my children are old enough to enter school. I feel that the factor most likely to influence this will be income. If my husband's income is adequate and we are able to manage smoothly on one income, I will remain home with my children. I really believe it is important to remain home to care for them. I would only return to work if financial reasons gave me no choice.

Perceptions of financial need play a greater role than actual income. While we do not know very much about particular life-style choices, such as whether they own their own houses, Homemakers make do on less family income to support their preference for staying home with their children. In contrast to the Careerists, this Homemaker's comment speaks for others: "My husband's income is enough to support the household and we have a small nest egg to fall back on. He was willing to become the sole breadwinner so that I could stay home."

Husbands of Homemakers do spend more time at work, on average about six hours a week longer, than men married to women in other groups (see Appendix, Table A.1). As some researchers report, perhaps husbands of nonemployed wives involve themselves more deeply in their jobs, and are not under pressure to share in family responsibilities such as leaving work early to pick up their children at a baby sitter.[1] Given the traditional division of labor in their families, they may feel freer to work longer hours, and to socialize at work, than men married to Careerists. A second explanation is, that as sole breadwinners, these men may feel they need to put in more hours in order to keep their jobs, given the corporate layoffs and extra work assigned to those who still hold jobs.

Couples in the Homemaker group use several strategies to achieve their goal of living on one income. They often use financial planning for contingencies as an essential component of their decision making. For example, Sally told us:

We sat down and went through everything that could happen if I didn't work. We figured out all our finances and decided that we had enough money to live on for six months in an emergency. We decided that this was enough so I would stay home.

Sometimes, Homemakers do without things they consider important, but they believe this trade-off is worth not returning to work after childbirth. Says one woman, "I don't want someone else to raise my children during the crucial formative years. I would prefer to sacrifice monetary comforts to raise them myself."

Other Homemakers develop alternatives or fall-back plans to get through financial emergencies. Jane says, "I knew we could barely get by on just my husband's salary, but we had some savings we could dip into when the kids are in school. I could ask my parents to help out if necessary." When asked how old she thinks a child should be for his or her mother to start working, she replies, "I think a mother should be home with her child for as long as she is financially able."

In summary, on the one hand, Homemakers believe that their husbands earn enough to support a family comfortably; on the other hand, Homemakers fulfill the traditional wife role and choose to go without material extras that their own income might otherwise provide in order to have a home with the proper family-centered atmosphere: A positive attitude toward family and plenty of time to be with their children.

CHILD CONCERNS

Perhaps Homemakers distinguish themselves most from the other groups—both as college students and a decade later as adults—by their concern with mothering. In fact, of all items in the survey that differentiate

Homemakers from the other groups, about 80 percent fall into the category of mothering (see Appendix, Table A.4 and Table 4.3). These women consistently express a desire to do the right thing for their children, to develop the best environment, and to provide for their children's security and happiness.

In college, many Homemakers reported childrearing strategies containing idealistic thinking, in which their children, mostly male, would be perfect people living in a perfect home and world. Their childrearing plans sounded more like dreams than plans.

Mother-Trained Children

In spite of the lack of experience apparent in their college dreams, now most Homemakers actually feel they have achieved what they desired for themselves and their children. As adults, Homemakers try to live up to this ideal by staying at home to mother full time. Florence, a former physical therapist, explains it this way:

After the birth of my first child, I felt a strong sense of commitment to being with her, enjoying her early years fully, and providing her with a secure, stimulating, loving environment. These feelings were very primal, not at all intellectual or rational. After the birth of my second child, my desire to return to work quickly has diminished even more. The overriding factors in my choice have been my desire to provide a quality environment for my children and my own "gut" feeling that I want to be with them.

Over time, women like Florence came to believe even more strongly in the path they had chosen. Compared to their views as students, adult experiences made them realize they would be even less likely to train their children themselves, or give their children enough attention, if they worked outside the home (see Table 4.3).

Socioemotional Development

In comparison to Careerists, Homemakers, as students and as adults, believe that continuing in the paid work force would result in their child feeling less secure, less loved, less disciplined, and less sociable. Says one Homemaker, "I felt that I could always get another job but I wouldn't be able to buy back the time. My oldest child is now three and I see a very independent, self-assured little girl. I've done my work in making her that way." As Mary Anne, a former merchandising assistant for a large department store chain, explains, "I believe that a preschooler needs the close contact of a full-time mother to be secure, loved, and disciplined. I did not want to leave the discipline and training of my child to others."

As adults, fewer Homemakers than Careerists think their children would do better in school if they work. They continue to believe in the negative effects of their working even as their children move out of infancy and toddlerhood and into the school system. They also believe more strongly than they did as college students that if they stay home, their children will be secure, well disciplined, and more sociable.

Instilling Family-Centered Values

Many Homemakers want to instill a family-centered life style in their children as much as they want to support their children's socioemotional development. Homemakers seem untouched by the changes in opportunities for women and the sex role changes of the 1980s. What they see, they do not like and do not want to emulate.

Many Homemakers of this generation consider their life-style a family tradition they are proud to perpetuate. They model their lives after the lives of their mothers just as the Careerists did. As Jeanne, formerly a customer service representative at a bank, explains:

I considered all of the firsts in a child's discipline and how I wanted my child to be disciplined. I wanted my child to be raised like I was. My husband and I talked many hours about these factors and others and basically about how we wanted our child to be raised and in what type of environment. We talked about our childhood upbringing and we both came to the same conclusion—that by our standards, it would be better for me to stay home with our child.

Quite a few Homemakers value their special role as the only ones able to instill their own set of moral, religious and/or spiritual values into their children. As Mary Anne, the former merchandising assistant, tells us:

My religious values are important to me and I wanted to be sure to instill them in my child. Actually, we never really made the decision for me to stop working when our child was born. It was assumed by both of us that I would become a full-time homemaker, probably because of the religious values we share.

In some cases, the strong family-centered beliefs by which these women guide their lives combine all three issues: Having healthier, better adjusted children, adhering to a particular family tradition, and inculcating particular moral and/or spiritual values in their children.

Undesirable Child Care Options

Given these values, Homemakers believe mothering should not be left to day care workers (see Appendix, Table A.4). As adults, they feel even more strongly than they did as students that if they were employed, their children would not receive enough attention when they needed it. They usually do not deny that adequate day care exists, but they do not desire this alternative for themselves. According to Cindi, a former claims adjuster, now home with her three-year-old daughter, "Children grow and change so much in the first five years of life. I don't want to miss my chance to help shape them into the kind of people I want them to be. Issues of self-esteem and basic trust are too important to leave to day care workers."

Even the availability of good child care would not change their lives. Fewer Homemakers than Nesters—the other stay-at-home group—say they would return to work if they had adequate child care. Nevertheless, while availability of good child care does not tempt them to return to work, they believe very strongly that competent, affordable day care should be available for those women who want it. They, themselves, however, now want a career in the home, not in the paid labor force they participated in before their children were born.

EMPLOYMENT CONCERNS SINCE COLLEGE

Homemakers never much wanted to have a career in the paid labor force. Indeed, among the four groups, they scored lowest on every career-related value item as college students, and even after having spent up to a decade in the paid work force before having a baby, they still do not visualize paid work as important (see Table 4.2). As college students, many Homemakers answered questions about their careers by discussing their family plans. As Nancy, a former social worker, explained when asked to describe her career strategy:

I really want to be a mother—to be there day in and day out. I want to be the one to nurture them—feed and change them—teach them about our world and watch with amazement how they learn things and interpret the world around them.

Employment Preparation

The Homemakers share traditional sex role beliefs common during their childhood, and their early experiences were unlikely to change their belief systems (see Appendix, Table A.1). On average, Homemakers were less likely to be firstborns than the women in the other groups. Researchers find that later-born children strive less for success, need achievement less, and value careers less highly. Consequently, Homemaker results resemble findings common to later-born children.[2]

Homemakers finished their baccalaureate education while working for pay fewer hours as students, and most often did not pursue an advanced degree. Homemakers may have done so because they did not commit to a continuous career, but they also limited their options for certain kinds of higher paying, intrinsically rewarding jobs. Thus, not surprisingly, fewer Homemakers became lawyers, doctors, and scientists—occupations that opened more to women while they attended school (see Appendix, Table A.1).

Negative Employment Experiences

As they entered the work force, Homemakers expected less and obtained lower-status jobs than Careerists. For example, they were far more likely to take service or "female ghetto" jobs requiring lower skill, offering lower pay, and not leading toward upwardly mobile career ladders. Consistent with being employed in a less desirable job, over 80 percent of the Homemakers left their first job within two years, a considerably greater percentage than women in the three other groups. Compared to the Careerists, however, fewer Homemakers would leave a job because it offered "no opportunity to progress" (see Appendix, Table A.3). Given their limited interest in such issues as career advancement, perhaps many Homemakers just marked time until childbirth. This is consistent with other studies finding that family-oriented men and women are less willing than career-oriented men and women to extend extra effort at work and receive lower merit increases.[3]

Even if they worked for pay mostly in deadend jobs, Homemakers did not see this as a problem, because their primary work was taking care of their families. As Judy, an administrative assistant for the Department of Labor, explains:

It seemed like an easy decision for me to leave my job after the baby was born. I do not particularly "enjoy" working—I was doing it to earn money, not because I had a career goal in mind. Also, I could not *begin* to compare my relationship with my children to the added luxuries working would provide.

As adults, Homemakers like Judy don't like the tradeoffs they would have to make in order to work—the benefits of paid work pale beside the costs of relinquishing their traditional role and having someone else raise

their children. As Susan, a marketing research analyst, puts it: "A child
needs to identify with parents during the first two years, and I'm not that
neurotic about forgoing a few years of career advancement to be with my
baby."

Like the Careerists, Homemakers do not view paid work as a source of
identity. In fact, they view employment as a negative. For instance, compared to the Careerists, fewer Homemakers see working as fun or as
providing a sense of accomplishment; in fact they feel more guilty and
resentful if they have to remain in the work force. Compared to when they
were in college, more Homemakers now would feel bored, tired, and have
less fun if they were pursuing careers (see Table 4.3). For the most part,
Homemakers hold these beliefs because they have had uninspiring experiences in the workplace, they have long held a positive view that a mother
is best suited to care for her child, and they do not see employment careers
as interesting.

Clearly, most Homemakers do not wish to be in the workplace—except
under duress—nor do they value careers. They also show little ambivalence
about these feelings. Yet even among this group, differences exist. A few
women still work, but under ten hours per week, thus keeping them from
being classified as Breadwinners. As Bernice puts it:

I did not need to work to earn money. I work at home and have been working through
the past five years but only for five to ten hours a week, so child care arrangements
have been fairly easy to make. Also, my hours are extremely flexible and I've
sometimes worked when the children have been sleeping. My work is more like a
hobby that I get paid for and enjoy. I do plan to increase my time working as the
children get older. But I wouldn't want to work more than part time until my
children were teenagers.

But what about their future? Many Homemakers believe they will have
sequential careers and return to paid work when their children are much
older. The comments of Charlotte, the mother of a six-year-old son and a
three-year-old daughter, sum up this attitude:

I wanted to raise my child and not have someone tell me what they did—I want it
all—in stages. Their formative years are very important, and since I will be 32 years
old when returning to the work force (full time), I'll still have plenty of time for
me.

Because researchers who examine the time between childbirth and return
to work find more work difficulties for those who wait longer to return,
Charlotte and other women like her may need additional training to achieve

their goals.[4] Homemakers may be the group that benefits most from programs designed to help reentry women.

SELF CONCERNS

As we examine how the Homemakers feel about themselves, we see a mixed picture. While they are positive about their lives at the present time, there are some cautionary signals for the future (see Appendix, Table A.5).

Pride in Family

Our data indicate that Homemakers are proud of their jobs as homemakers and loyal to their profession in much the same way Careerists are loyal to theirs. Taking responsibility for raising their children primarily shapes this loyalty and pride. Since their values are consistent with their life-style, they feel satisfied with their lives.

Homemakers' identity and sense of mastery derive from their home and childrearing. In their book, *Lifeprints*, Grace Baruch and her associates write of women who stay home to care for their families as achieving a sense of mastery if they actually like the work they do.[5] That is, the more women find that homemaking involves the kind of work they enjoy and are good at, the higher their sense of mastery. In our study as well, most Homemakers enjoy a feeling of mastery and competence derived from liking what they do. Indeed, homemaking functions for Homemakers as paid work does for the Careerists—engaging their skills and providing a sense of pride and self-worth. They have made a conscious decision that, at least for now, they best meet their own needs and those of their families by remaining out of the paid work force.

They display a sense of mastery and competence from this choice derived from having control over their lives. On the whole, the Homemakers have been able to follow the path that is consistent with their value system. Not surprisingly, their scores indicate a healthy self-concept (see Table A.5). Their inner strength, manifested by clear beliefs and values, as well as spouses who generally share and support these values, enable them to go against prevailing norms in a society where the majority of women return to work shortly after childbirth.

Yet Homemakers may face a cloudy future. From a practical view, few Homemakers feel they have enough time for themselves even though they do not do paid work. Compared to when they were in college, they are significantly more likely to associate "feeling tired" and "feeling tied down" with being homemakers. They believe that time for themselves can wait until they do not have young children at home. Since numerous studies report that full-time homemakers have lower levels of physical and mental well-being compared to employed mothers, Homemakers need to attend to these feelings. Homemakers may feel even more fatigued as their children get older.

One recent study by Ravenna Helson and her associates at Berkeley looks at women over a fourteen-year period.[6] In the first year, very few differences were found between women who had not married, women who resumed their careers after their children were born, and women who remained homemakers. However, by the time the women were in their early forties (e. g., Year 14 of their study), Homemakers had more psychosomatic complaints and lower levels of well-being compared to the other groups. By comparison, the women who combined paid work and motherhood felt fatigued but healthy.

Homemakers face another potential problem because they depend so much on their husbands' approval of their current life-style. Since their partnership depends upon maintaining a traditional division of labor, when their children are older and more self-sufficient, the current equilibrium and balance in their relationships may disappear. Thus, if these women choose to enter the paid labor force as their children age, they may need to renegotiate a long-standing marital contract—a process that is often difficult and painful.

Third, Homemakers realistically recognize personal costs in giving up career prospects, but they rarely acknowledge how much their security depends upon the earning capacity and health of their spouses. For instance, as adults, more Homemakers understand that they have given up career advancement and job contacts by not working. Should they wish to resume paid work in the future, they believe they will be able to select from a wide array of available options including assuming part-time jobs, going back to school, trying second careers, undertaking substantive volunteer work, and starting their own businesses. Few anticipate widowhood, spouse unemployment, or "reentry" problems that may require counseling or additional training before they can assume the role of family breadwinner.

CONCLUSION

Homemakers believe their lives are working out well. They have made a conscious decision that for this time in their lives, they best meet their own needs, as well as their family's needs, by staying out of the paid work force.

As far back as college, or even earlier, they did not value careers in the paid labor force highly. They raise their children in accordance with their beliefs that no one can take the place of a mother. They married spouses who share their traditional sex role ideology and gain satisfaction from this congruence of values. Although the Homemakers now feel a little more tired and tied down than they had anticipated, they accept this, because they are committed to what they are doing and they enjoy domesticity.

Unlike the other groups in the study, Homemakers willingly make financial sacrifices in total family income in order to maintain this life-style. In turn, they believe they provide a secure and warm environment where they are always available for their children and produce healthy well-adjusted children who will believe in their own value system and morality. This reduces any ambivalence they might otherwise feel from the conflicting social cues supporting both family values and employed mothers.

Overall, these women are very satisfied with their lives, show little anxiety, and have a healthy self-concept tied to their identities as mothers and home managers. In the future, as responsibilities for their children diminish, many plan to rejoin the paid labor force. Others who truly like the work of homemaking (apart from childrearing) may choose to stay home. Having the choice—having clear priorities and being able to continue to live according to their preferences within the ambiguous social environment—maintains their sense of well-being and reduces ambivalence.

NOTES

1. G. Farkas. (1976). Education, wage rates and the division of labor between husband and wife. *Journal of Marriage and the Family*, *39*, 473–483.

2. R. B. Zajonc & G. B. Markus. (1975). Birth order and intellectual development. *Psychological Review*, *82*, 74–88; M. Hennig & A. Jardin. (1977). *The managerial woman*. Garden City, NY: Anchor Press/Doubleday.

3. S. A. Lobel & L. St. Clair. (1992). Effects of family responsibilities, gender, and career identity salience on performance outcomes. *Academy of Management Journal*, *35*, 1057–1069.

4. M. K. Wadman. (1992). Mothers who take extended time off find their careers pay a heavy price. *Wall Street Journal*, July 16, B1, B5.

5. G. Baruch, R. Barnett, & C. Rivers. (1983). *Lifeprints: New patterns of love and work for today's women*. New York: McGraw-Hill.

6. R. Helson & J. Picano. (1990). Is the traditional role bad for women? *Journal of Personality and Social Psychology*, *59*, 311–320.

Chapter 5

Breadwinners

Sally, a woman who in college thought she would stay home after childbirth, describes her decision to return to work after she gave birth to her first child:

It all boils down to MONEY. Can I afford to stay home with mortgage, car, and student loan payments? The only other factors that affect my decision are availability of good child care and how my career is going.

My major counsels in this decision are my husband and our accountant because I don't want to end up baby-poor. We really have to review our financial position. I would not be willing to forgo my salary, because I feel that it is important for a child to have a certain standard of living. I would also like child care at the office so I could use lunch time to be with my child.

The Careerists and Homemakers discussed in the previous chapters present a stable pattern—life has turned out pretty much the way they wanted it to in college. By comparison Breadwinners like Sally present a pattern of change. The "life scripts" they created in college altered dramatically. They started out with many of the values and plans of Homemakers, but within a decade after graduating from college, the Breadwinners came to resemble the Careerists. As students, like the Homemakers, the Breadwinners believed "mothers belong at home." They did not aspire to careers or intend to return to paid work after childbirth. However, by Phase II of our study, they had made a 180-degree turn, and their life-styles now include working for pay after childbirth.

What caused these profound changes in the Breadwinners' lives? Primarily, the changes stem from their pragmatic adaptation to events around them. Of all of the groups in our study, changing economic and social conditions seem to have had the most dramatic impact on their lives. Commitment to either career advancement or domesticity as a part of their identities did not fuel these changes. Because their identities were not tied to a particular role, they responded with pragmatic flexibility and based their decisions on their need for income and pride in earning money for their families.

Their own growing independence and confidence as adults accentuate these changes. Breadwinners have come to realize that, in contrast to their earlier views, they can manage to work for pay *and* care for their families. They accept that their children will do as well, if not better, if they work for pay rather than stay home. Yet almost with one voice, they call for better day care and organizational cultures more sympathetic to employed mothers.

EMPLOYMENT CONCERNS

Breadwinners matured into life-styles different from those of their parents, confronting the economic needs of their families and working out a compromise that enables them to earn needed income and relish their jobs. In the context of this compromise, many of them work part time, or as little or as much as they need to survive economically. Others work as little or as much as they need to survive emotionally (see Appendix, Table A.1).

Employment Preparation

More than women in the three other groups, Breadwinners come from traditional middle-class families living in small towns or suburbs. Their fathers obtained the most education of the four sets of parents—more than half have college degrees. Fewer Breadwinners' mothers than Careerists' mothers worked when their children were young (see Appendix, Table A.1). Most Breadwinners grew up in the "typical" suburban life-style during the 1970s where women worked until they had children, then "retired" to raise them, and returned to paid work when their children were adolescents Not surprisingly, therefore, Breadwinners did not expect to return to work after childbirth.

Changing norms, which increased acceptability for mothers of young children to work for pay, are mirrored in the Breadwinners' attitudes, values, and their decisions to continue working for pay after they had children. Interestingly, more mothers and best friends now support their daughters' employment than when Breadwinners were students. Also, now Breadwinners are more willing to go against their father's wishes if he does not approve. The combination of changing social norms, growing maternal approval, and increasing independence made it easier for the Breadwinners to believe that they could combine paid work and family responsibilities (see Table 5.1).

The Importance of Income

For many Breadwinners, income motivates them most to return to paid work after childbirth. Thus, having enough family income is highly valued at both time periods (see Table 5.2). Living on two salaries has become common—perhaps necessary—for the majority of young families by the early 1990s. More Breadwinners than Homemakers now believe that if they stay home they will not have enough family income or extra income, making it necessary for their husbands to hold two jobs (see Table 5.3 and Table 4.3). However, on average, their husbands do not earn less than the Homemakers' husbands. So, without the Homemaker's strong family-centered ideology of "a mother's place is in the home," the more pragmatic Breadwinners develop a strategy to provide their desired income and balance paid work and homemaking after their children are born.

Beth, an administrator at a small manufacturing company, expresses some of these concerns: "My decision to return to work is based on family income needed in order to meet the bills *and* provide *some* luxuries. We

Table 5.1
Breadwinners' Perceptions of Approval of and Compliance with Referents

	Phase I		Phase II	
	Approval[d]	Compliance[e]	Approval[d]	Compliance[e]
1. Mother	2.87[a],*	3.09	3.40*	2.49
2. Father	2.76	3.03*	3.08	2.59*
3. Husband	3.06[a]	4.04	3.91[b]	3.78
4. Best Friend	3.62*	2.84	3.94*	2.53
5. Boss	---	---	3.33[a,c]	3.94
6. Co-worker	---	---	3.47[a,c]	4.66

*Phase I significantly different from Phase II
[a]Significantly different from Careerists, $p > .05$
[b]Significantly different from Homemakers, $p > .05$
[c]Significantly different from Nesters, $p > .05$
[d]1=very likely to disapprove, 5=very likely to approve
[e]1=I am unlikely to do as they wish, 5=I am likely to do as they wish

Table 5.2
Values of Breadwinners

Values[d]	Phase I	Phase II
Having fun	4.30	4.37
A sense of accomplishment	4.63	4.72
Feeling tied down	1.86	1.89
Having variety in my life	3.90	4.00
Feeling guilty	1.28	1.16
Feeling resentful	1.70	1.07
Feeling tired	1.56	1.56
Feeling bored	1.35	1.41
Feeling close to my husband	4.82	4.90
Feeling close to my child	4.86	4.93
Running my household smoothly	3.99	3.97
Training my child myself	4.11	3.99[b]
Maintaining my career skills	4.30	3.89
Maintaining my job contacts	4.11[*]	3.76[b,*]
Advancing my career	3.93[*]	3.61[*]
Earning enough income myself	3.66[b]	3.58
Having enough family income	4.59	4.56
Having extra income	4.10	3.96
Making more $ than it costs		
me to work	4.16	4.42
Husband needing two jobs	1.28	1.56
Missing child's growth milestones	1.51	1.58
Finding adequate child care	3.89[a,b]	4.61[b]
Having enough time for the child	4.70	4.62
Having enough time for myself	4.35	4.38

Table 5.2 (continued)

	Phase I	Phase II
Values[d]		
Having enough time for my husband	4.68	4.49
Husband helping around the house	4.25	4.39
Child will be independent	4.08	4.30
Child will be secure	4.75	4.86
Child will be well disciplined	4.42	4.49
Child will get along easily with others	4.62	4.62
Child will learn beliefs	3.58	---
Child will feel loved	4.89	4.96
Child will have attention when needed	4.69	4.75
Child feels closer to others than to me	2.11	1.70
Child will believe women are competent	---	4.51
Child will do better in school	---	4.43

*Phase I significantly different from Phase II
[a]Significantly different from Careerists, $p > .05$
[b]Significantly different from Homemakers, $p > .05$
[c]Significantly different from Nesters, $p > .05$
[d]1=extremely undesirable, 5=extremely desirable

want to maintain a comparable standard of living." Nanette, a systems analyst explains,

My maternity leave was without pay. We did put money aside for a few months, but I needed to get back to work to secure my job. We need two incomes to live. I also have health benefits that my husband's job does not provide.

Similar thoughts are expressed by Barbara, an administrator employed by a large health care organization. Now on maternity leave, she tells us:

The most important factor by far was finances. Between my firm's maternity leave policy and my untaken vacation time, I had about four months of unpaid leave. My husband and I sat down and figured out how long we felt comfortable going without my salary and decided upon two months. Then I asked my firm for approximately six months off and they accommodated me. I'll be going back next month, four days per week.

Clearly, Breadwinners worry about managing to stay afloat without incurring too much debt. They are working for more than just "pin money" or to buy a few extras. However, they have earned *more* money than they thought they would. Although on average, Breadwinners do not earn more money than Careerists, more say their pay expectations have been met at work (see Appendix, Table A.2). Breadwinners' perceptions may reflect the proverbial case of the glass being half full. If, in college, Breadwinners did not have high career aspirations, and did not expect to return to work after childbirth, they may never have expected to earn much money as adults. So they have been able to meet or exceed their expectations not only for pay, but also for general enjoyment of work.

Work Is More Fun Than Expected

In part, Breadwinners return to work because employment has turned out to be a better experience than they anticipated in college (see Table 5.3). They now think employment will be more fun than they thought in Phase I. Compared to the Careerists, relatively few adult Breadwinners talk about commitment to work for pay as part of their identity or speak of serious career aspirations. More often, boredom at home and enjoyment of the workplace encourages them to return to work. Says Marilyn, a former marketing analyst for a large pharmaceutical company:

I went back to work a lot faster than I thought I would because I was so used to being out of the house 12–14 hours a day and now I was stuck home. I happened to read about a job in a local paper that looked like fun and I was able to take my daughter to the job with me, as the woman I worked for worked at home.

Compared to the other groups, the Breadwinners spent a longer time at their first jobs and many of the adult Breadwinners now say they find work interesting. Several research studies show that challenging jobs in an early career stage have a positive impact on employees.[1] For example, young employees given challenging assignments generally perform more effectively and are promoted faster than their counterparts who are not given as much challenge. Thus, initial positive experiences may have increased the perceived advantages of working among the Breadwinners.

Breadwinners also now resemble the Careerists in that both groups feel less guilty about employment than the Homemakers do. Yet they feel more guilty than they thought they would a decade earlier and they maintain the desire to give their families personal care. This leads many Breadwinners into part-time work arrangements.

Table 5.3

Breadwinners' Perceptions of the Consequences of Working and Not Working Following Childbirth

Consequences[d]	Phase I		Phase II	
	Working	Not Working	Working	Not Working
Having fun	3.48[*]	4.01[a]	3.73[b,*]	3.96
A sense of accomplishment	4.03	3.59[a]	4.21	3.42
Feeling tied down	2.74	2.89[*]	3.01	3.32[*]
Having variety in my life	3.61	3.06[a]	3.70	2.89[b]
Feeling guilty	2.99[*]	1.66[a,c]	3.54[b,*]	2.41
Feeling resentful	2.51[a]	2.14[a,c,*]	2.86	2.84[*]
Feeling tired	3.59	2.53[c,*]	4.21	3.04[*]
Feeling bored	2.13	2.68[a,c,*]	1.84	3.22[*]
Feeling close to my husband	3.67	4.44[*]	3.78[b]	4.17[*]
Feeling close to my child	3.46[a]	4.71	3.96[b]	4.61
Running my household smoothly	2.90	4.51	2.87	4.44
Training my child myself	2.71[c,*]	4.68	3.01[b,*]	4.79
Maintaining my career skills	4.39	2.79	4.20	1.94[c]
Maintaining my job contacts	4.37	2.61	4.24	1.99[c]
Advancing my career	4.21[*]	1.83	3.84[*]	1.42
Earning enough income myself	3.89	1.36	3.97	1.25
Having enough family income	4.29	3.35	4.49	2.49[b]
Having extra income	4.17	2.55	3.92	1.73[b]
Making more $ than it costs				
me to work	4.06	1.90[*]	4.28	1.50[*]
Husband needing two jobs	1.33	2.10[a,*]	1.31	2.66[b,*]
Missing child's growth milestones	3.20[a]	1.45	3.20[b]	1.68
Finding adequate child care	3.67	3.32[*]	3.93[b]	2.68[*]

Table 5.3 (Continued)

	Phase I		Phase II	
Consequences[d]	Working	Not Working	Working	Not Working
Having enough time for the child	3.07	4.71	3.10[b]	4.54
Having enough time for myself	2.69	4.30*	2.35[b]	4.03*
Having enough time for my husband	3.07	4.51	2.74[b]	4.28
Husband helping around the house	4.20	3.26	4.06	2.94
Child will be independent	3.91	3.74	3.89	3.63
Child will be secure	3.55[a]	4.54	3.80[b]	4.42
Child will be well disciplined	3.49[a]	4.51[c]	3.73[b]	4.42
Child will get along easily with others	3.87[a]	4.26	4.13[b]	4.16[a]
Child will learn beliefs	3.1	3.96	---	---
Child will feel loved	4.16	4.78	4.36[b]	4.96
Child will have attention when				
needed	3.57	4.65	3.73[b]	4.62
Child feels closer to others				
than to me	3.22*	2.39	2.76*	2.13
Child will believe women are				
competent	---	---	4.04	3.82
Child will do better in school	---	---	3.51[b]	3.97

*Phase I significantly different from Phase II
[a]Significantly different from Careerists, $p > .05$
[b]Significantly different from Homemakers, $p > .05$
[c]Significantly different from Nesters, $p > .05$
[d]1=very unlikely, 5=very likely

A Part-Time Workable Compromise

Like the Careerists, some Breadwinners view temporary part-time work as a way of maintaining good child care without sacrificing advancement or, more importantly, salary. Compared to women in other groups, Bread-winners see employment similarly in some ways but also significantly different in others. For example, when Careerists choose part-time work, they are more likely to view it as a *temporary* situation before resuming their careers. While the Breadwinners may negotiate a life-style choice dictated by economic changes, many prefer part-time employment to full-time work or to full-time homemaking. Brenda works as a representative for a major insurance company that sells benefit packages to corporations. She says:

The only way I would agree to return to work after my child was born was on a part-time basis but still offering the same responsibilities and salary rate. Also, prior to my child, my job required quite a bit of overnight travel. My company realigned my territory so I do not have to spend nights away. Remarkably, if I do need to travel, the company pays all expenses so that my son and nanny can accompany me. (My husband and I discussed what would be acceptable job parameters. I relayed that to my boss and human resources manager and we came to the above job description.)

Most commonly, economic factors converge with part-time employment as a way to maintain satisfactory child welfare and an acceptable family standard of living.

Both Celeste and Suzanne possess strategies for reaching a workable balance typical of many Breadwinners. Celeste, a youth group worker, notes that she chose to return to work quickly after the birth of her child primarily because of economic factors. Also, she says:

My situation is different because I had a full-time job and a part-time job before our son was born. My part-time job of teaching aerobics was like a hobby that I got paid for. Now I've expanded this job and returned to it because I can accommodate my hours to my son's schedule because my son can stay with me at the health club where I work.

Suzanne, now pregnant with her first child, says:

If I find myself getting bored or restless and wanting adult conversation after about six months, I will definitely work part time. If no good child care is available, I will try to encourage my present boss to let me work out of my home.

Changing opportunity structures in the decade between Phase I and Phase II, combined with their collegiate educational backgrounds, benefitted the Breadwinners whether they chose careers or part-time jobs. The Breadwinners stay in the labor force, not because of long-held views and values common among Careerists and Homemakers, but because they responded to social and economic changes. At the same time, they have managed to keep their beliefs that children must be well cared for while arranging to share these responsibilities with others.

HOME CONCERNS

Breadwinners lack the strong family-centered values and traditional domestic commitment of Homemakers. A philosophy of life influenced by pragmatic adaptation to societal changes rather than Homemakers' commitment to exclusive maternal care enabled them to shift patterns and beliefs in adulthood (see Appendix, Table A.4). This shift is characterized by increased confidence that they can manage at home while they work outside of the home. Specifically, now they believe they will have enough time for their families, and their spouses will agree to their working.

Time Management

In the decade between Phase I and Phase II, the Breadwinners came to believe there was enough time to continue working and still maintain the quality of their relationships with their husbands and children. In Phase II they are more likely, than when they were students, to believe that they can train their children themselves and that their children will feel close to them while they are working. They also are somewhat *less* likely to believe they will feel closer to their husbands if not working than they believed as students. As Beth, the administrator, notes:

We also want to provide enough time for our child in order to at least supplement, if not provide, the best environment both emotionally and educationally toward her development. It is also very important for me to have enough time for my husband   • to maintain our relationship and to have time for our family.

As they plan their time management strategies, Breadwinners value the opportunity to work flexible or part-time hours when their children are very young. Brenda, who takes her son along with her when she has to travel, observes:

My employer continued to offer me challenging work and reward me according to my performance. Also, I could devote more time to my family than if I worked full time all year long. On the other hand, an inflexible attitude on the part of my employer would have caused me to leave.

Attitude Toward Domesticity

Part of their adult beliefs that they will have enough time to combine employment and homemaking comes from Breadwinners changing their attitudes toward being homemakers. As college students, the Breadwinners shared views that were very similar to those of the Homemakers. Compared to the Careerists, both groups thought staying home after childbirth would be a positive experience—fun and challenging and not generally producing guilt, resentment, and boredom. However, the Breadwinners no longer feel this way. Instead, they resent staying home full time and associate *no* paid employment after childbirth with feeling bored, tired, and tied down (see Table 5.3 and Appendix, Table A.4). Yet, they make fewer condescending comments about finding domesticity tedious or not wanting to be "Suzy Homemaker" than the Careerists do. Nor do they identify themselves as the guardians of "family values," extolling the virtues of homemaking as do the Homemakers.

This moderate approach is consistent with their pragmatic self-concept. From a practical viewpoint, not letting their identity be defined by either role may allow Breadwinners to budget their time appropriately and enable them to get on with domestic responsibilities. But they no longer associate positive outcomes with full-time domesticity.

Supportive Spouses

As college students, Breadwinners believed that by not working they would feel closer to their spouses. A decade later they are less likely to believe this (see Table 5.3). Why the change? Their husbands clearly approve of their working outside the home (see Table 5.1). But, more importantly for this group, family finances influence the change. Recall that Barbara, the health administrator, made a joint decision with her husband based on financial considerations. And Nanette, the systems analyst, returned not only because her income is needed, but because her health care benefits are needed as well. By returning to paid work after childbirth, Breadwinners reduce pressure on their husbands to be the sole wage earner. As Lynn, an auditor, puts it, "$ is the number 1 reason I returned to work. To keep us moving toward our financial goals, I need to work." Similar thoughts are echoed by Sherry, who says, "If my husband's income were enough so that we could all live comfortably, I'd stay home." Like most Breadwinners, these women now believe that if they do not earn money, they would not have a sufficient family income for their husbands to work only one job.

The Breadwinners may associate their working for pay with feeling close to their husbands for another reason. Their spouses work the fewest hours— on average six hours less than the Homemakers' husbands (see Appendix, Table A.1). So perhaps wives' employment enables these couples to spend more time together. As Carrie says:

My husband and I decided that it was very important to our marriage to have some time together. We felt if he took a second job, we would have little or no time together.

Now, because it frees their husbands from income-producing demands, Breadwinners are confident that their employment brings benefits both to their husbands and to their children.

CHILD CONCERNS

In an intriguing shift, the Breadwinners reversed their concerns that their children would suffer negative consequences if they worked outside the home. Breadwinners now believe their employment will have a positive influence on their children's development, in part, because they have put more trust in effective child care (see Table 5.3). As college students, however, they were more likely to believe they would have adequate child care if they were *not* working. Their beliefs about the effects of working on children, which were significantly different from those of Careerists in Phase I, are now significantly different from those of Homemakers.

Missing Milestones

As college students, Breadwinners feared they would not experience the pleasures of motherhood if they worked away from home. They believed that if they were employed, their children would come to feel closer to others than to themselves. Also, compared to Careerists, they feared that employment might prevent them from sharing their children's growth milestones (e.g., first steps, first words) on a daily basis (Table 5.3).

Now, although they are responding with the same scores, they differ from Homemakers. Mainly, Breadwinner mothers arrange their time so that they can still play an essential role in rasing their children. Brenda says:

I considered the following factors: Having time for my husband and child and training my child the way my husband and I wish to instill moral and spiritual values that may not be done outside the home as well as we want them instilled. The other factors are work opportunities such as a flexible part-time work schedule—either at my present full-time job or work elsewhere; my financial situation, my desire to have my family and household run as harmoniously as possible; and my desire to maintain my career skills.

Nan, still anticipating the decision whether to stay home or return to work, says:

My employer could continue to offer me challenging work and reward me according to my performance. If they offered me part-time work, I'd seriously consider staying after the baby is born. On the other hand, inflexible attitudes by my employer would make me more inclined to stay home. I also presently hold a second (part-time) job as a CPA during tax season, which could very likely turn into flexible seasonal work during motherhood. This would allow me to devote more time to family than if I worked full-time all year long.

Often women struggle when they try to arrange their schedules and work lives to leave more time for their families. One mother, disgusted with the lack of flexibility on the part of her employer, reports:

Staying at home full time for five months worked well for me. I was still breast-feeding, but also used supplemental formula. I wouldn't have wanted to wean the baby any sooner. On-site child care would have been wonderful, also more emotional and moral support, and more standardization of maternity benefits. This is a male-dominated company and it shows.

Others more successfully negotiate time flexibility with their employers:

Forcing me to come back earlier would have resulted in my resignation. I had three months off and three months part time. Only at that point did I feel ready to work full time. Any earlier, and the decision would have been to stay home with my daughter.

Having chosen to return to work after childbirth, Breadwinners now share the Careerists' views that they can train their children themselves even if they are working. These women now believe they can combine successful, competent mothering with paid work as long as they have a reasonably accommodating employer. If their employers do not help, Breadwinners find alternative resources to ensure that their children thrive or consider part-time work, or other employers.

Changing Child Development Beliefs

In college, Breadwinners believed that staying home was a way to raise happy, healthy, well-adjusted children. In fact, when asked what they thought was the appropriate age for a mother to return to work, both Homemakers and Breadwinners gave virtually identical answers: "When a child starts school." But as we have seen in many other areas, their views shifted as adults and now mirror those of the Careerists. By Phase II of our study, Breadwinners associate only positive effects with their working outside the home: Children will be more secure, disciplined, sociable, and loved. Like the Careerists, and unlike the Homemakers, they also believe their children will do as well in school if they, themselves, are employed (see Table 5.3).

Because we surveyed and interviewed these women only twice in a ten-year period, we do not know for sure what influenced these changes. Did they reevaluate their views on the negative effects and then decide to continue their careers? Or did they return to paid work and then reevaluate their views? We do have one clue to answer these questions: Because Breadwinners who have not yet had children also now believe their employment will benefit their children, it seems likely that the women in this group reevaluated their choices before they had children. This may be their response to shifting cultural norms or to the realities of family budgetary needs and employer policies. Changing opinions about child care also might have weighed heavily in their decisions.

Changing Child Care Beliefs

Even more striking than the shift in the Breadwinners' beliefs about the effects of their working on their children's growth and socioemotional development, Breadwinners shifted their beliefs about child care. Unlike the Homemakers, they now believe that exclusive maternal care is not what they want or need for their children (see Appendix, Table A.4). Florence, a special education teacher, notes:

Money was a factor in returning to work since my income was a considerable percentage of our family income. However, we were willing to sacrifice more family income if we couldn't find child care we were comfortable with. We didn't want to utilize day care for an infant, so finding the right caregiver was vitally important for my returning to work.

Says Jacqueline, an intensive care nurse who has not yet had a child:

My primary consideration will be availability of quality day care. If it's not available, I may only work part time. If it is available, I'll be free to concentrate on work during the work day. But I don't want to go back too quickly. About six months after having a baby would be fine.

The Breadwinners use a variety of strategies to obtain satisfactory child care—day care centers, friends, and relatives all play a part. Leslie, a speech therapist who returned to work when her baby was seven months old, speaks about her child care this way: "An old family friend is baby sitting while I work. I am confident with her and she also has children of her own for our son to play with." Lisa, a freelance editor, tells us:

I was able to return to work on a freelance basis without worrying about my son's care as he was babysat [sic] by my parents. If I had to find child care and pay for it, I would have waited longer to return. Also, we needed my money to pay for our mortgage.

Naturally, many women worried about the quality of their child care, especially for infants. Betsy, the manager of a children's clothing store, says:

The lack of quality child care influenced me to stay home for 2-1/2 years after the baby was born. Although our household income was stretched to the limit, we did not want to sacrifice our child's well-being. Also, we agreed the high cost of child care was not worth it, as it would eat up most of the money I made from working. But as this was our firstborn, no one was really good enough.

Although concern for infant care remains, Breadwinners changed their minds regarding the acceptability of having someone other than themselves care for their small children. Like most women, they view obtaining child care as their responsibility, but they look for companies with good benefits to enable them to do this. In contrast to ten years ago, they now earn enough money to purchase adequate care, and sometimes they even find companies that offer some, if not all, of the benefits they desire. Sally, in the opening scenario, said her company has a referral service, flex hours, and is very accommodating, overall. But she still believes on-site child care would be a big plus.

Like Sally, most Breadwinners and other women consider on-site child care a great idea. Some would like to see flexible spending accounts reimbursing parents for day care as well. The combination of good care by others and their own beliefs that they can still stay in touch with their children supports the life-style they have chosen.

SELF CONCERNS

On the whole, the Breadwinners seem content with their lives. Contrary to their expectations in college, they enjoy working. They appear happy, healthy and satisfied by the rewards and excitement of a busy life. Like the Careerists and Homemakers, they now score high on the scale measuring self-confidence and competence, suggesting that they feel in control of their lives (see Appendix, Table A.5).

Balance and Pride in Unexpected Income

Why are these women, who have added the role of paid worker to the roles of wife and mother, so well off? Clearly, the Breadwinners often feel overloaded. But, they value the income as well as the equilibrium and balance that employment brings to their lives and they are not as confident now, as they were as college students, that if they stayed home they would have enough time for themselves. In addition, they believe the rewards far outweigh the costs. The variety and complexity of the Breadwinners' jobs give them new vitality. Also, they feel a sense of control over their lives in choosing to reverse their college plans. Finally, they have much support for their choices from those close to them—spouses, mothers, friends, and bosses. At a societal level, changing social norms put them "in sync" with the times: They do not feel they are swimming against the tide.

Some theorists give another explanation for Breadwinners' general sense of satisfaction.[2] Traditionally, most people think that adding a role creates more work and greater likelihood of problems and stress. But others believe that energy expands as individuals *choose* to take on another role—"If you want something done, give it to a busy person."

Consistent with this line of reasoning, when women take on an additional role, particularly paid work, they may eliminate or avoid doing tasks they dislike. For example, Elise, mother of a three-year-old, tells us:

During the six months I stayed home, I was the only one "at home" among a large extended family of sisters, brothers, and assorted in-laws who live nearby. They expected all sorts of favors from me. They often had their purchases sent to me because they knew I would be home. And they expected me to run various errands for them.

Now back working at her accounting job, Elise no longer has to contend with such requests. Her paid job is the excuse not to have to do family jobs she did not want to do in the first place.

Multiple roles may also serve as buffers for each other.[3] That is, after a long hard day at a paid job, coming home to a family can provide pleasure and contentment. The reverse is true as well. "Escaping" from a draining day at home can also be pleasurable. As Breadwinners, these women enjoy both options.

Balance, control over their life choices, and social support contribute to Breadwinners' self-confidence. In addition, they may benefit from using home and employment roles to buffer and complement each other while escaping the more unpleasant aspects of each.

CONCLUSION

Although money may motivate the Breadwinners to remain in the paid work force, they enjoy their jobs. In contrast to what they envisioned as college students, they are more likely to equate feeling bored and resentful with the thought of staying home. In part, this stems from the realization that if they stay home, their family's standard of living would suffer and they wouldn't have enough time or money for themselves and their families. Breadwinners responded to the environmental ambiguity of changing social norms and reduced their ambivalence by pragmatically responding to social change.

While having a career does play a larger role in their lives than they anticipated in college, most Breadwinners remain uncommitted to achievement at work as a life goal. Thus advancement and maintaining job contacts interest Breadwinners less as adults than as students. They are now less likely as adults to believe that working will lead to career advancement than they were as students. Like the Careerists, they are willing to put their careers on hold for a while, but not permanently. Yet, they will leave their jobs for other jobs if there is no *opportunity* for mobility, so they do want some growth and opportunity eventually (see Appendix, Table A.3). But, unlike the Careerists, employment does not form the center of their identities.

As they gradually realized that they might not prefer the homemaker role, Breadwinners pragmatically acknowledged that doing something they did not enjoy might not benefit their children. They enact this belief with careful strategies about time management and child care, which enable them to keep in touch with their children's development and still maintain their employment. Many Breadwinners take part-time jobs and others select child care workers who particularly stimulate their trust. If their requirements cannot be met, they change employers or stay home until acceptable arrangements can be made. The freedom from an identity defined by one or the other of these choices enables them to use whichever strategy meets their current and long-term needs.

In addition to changing economic conditions, changing social norms and social support influenced the Breadwinners to veer away from their original course. They have surrounded themselves with friends and spouses who hold views similar to their own. Although they live complex, busy lives, with this support they find their life-style personally enriching and beneficial to their families' financial welfare and their own happiness.

NOTES

1. D. W. Bray, R. J. Campbell, & D. L. Grant. (1974). *Formative years in business: A long-term AT&T study of managerial lives.* New York: Wiley & Sons.

2. G. K. Baruch & R. Barnett. (1986). Role quality, multiple role involvement, and psychological well-being among midlife women. *Journal of Personality and Social Psychology, 51*, 578–585; P. Voydanoff & B. W. Donnelly. (1989). Work and family roles and psychological distress. *Journal of Marriage and the Family, 51*, 923–932.

3. F. Crosby. (1991). *Juggling: The unexpected advantage of balancing career and home for women and their families.* New York: The Free Press.

Chapter 6

Nesters

In college, Nora was sure she wanted to work for pay after childbirth, but in the end, she did not. She relates what happened as follows:

My husband's company relocated us from New Jersey to Florida in June. I had to leave my job on Wall Street. I tried for six months to obtain new employment in Florida but with no success. Since January, I have been disabled due to pregnancy complications, so I will remain unemployed. But even if I had been working all along, I would not have returned after the birth of my child because I've decided it is more important to me be a good mother than a good career woman. I didn't want my child raised with someone else's values, and I don't want to miss my child growing up.

Until about four years ago, I thought day care would not be a problem, but gradually I've changed my mind. I'm not comfortable with the thought of it. The move to Florida also made me feel more strongly about staying home because we have no family in the area to help with the baby sitting or to check and make sure everything is okay.

I miss working in some ways and I might decide to pursue a part-time job at some time in the future, but I'm not sure about the timetable. I might go back to school or maybe have another child. It's hard to make plans when you're not familiar with the community.

In contrast to the stability of the Careerists and the Homemakers, the lives of Nesters like Nora underwent significant change in adulthood. In the period between Phase I and Phase II, Nesters traded career aspirations for domesticity and full-time motherhood. They chose to interrupt their careers in order to raise their children. Were the changes due to a single life course event or did they result from a cumulative process that extended through the years?

The Nesters—the group who planned in college to have careers but then decided to become homemakers—were by far the smallest group in the study. Only 15 individuals make up this group—five women who already have a child and ten women who, although they do not have a child, intend to stay home when they do. The size of the group is an interesting commentary on the changes of the past decade. This small minority of women moved in the opposite direction from the national social trends encouraging women to work outside the home discussed in Chapter 1. The small group size also explains, in part, why fewer differences with other groups are statistically significant.

This chapter explains why Nesters turned toward domesticity and describes what distinguishes them from those who decided to continue to work outside the home after childbirth. In short, the Nesters met the environmental ambiguity with ambivalence. Nesters like paid work, but do not see it as central to their identity. More important to them is their husbands' approval. When they met with discouragement from bosses and co-workers, and experienced life events that made it difficult to work outside of the home (see Table 6.1), it was easier to give up a career, even though they personally preferred employment. However, they paid a price in self-confidence for this sacrifice.

Table 6.1
Nesters' Perceptions of Approval of and Compliance with Referents

	Phase I		Phase II	
	Approval[d]	Compliance[e]	Approval[d]	Compliance[e]
1. Mother	3.40	2.50	2.79	2.93
2. Father	3.33	2.71	2.93	2.64
3. Husband	3.81[b]	3.67	3.36	3.27
4. Best Friend	4.06	2.80	3.69	2.47
5. Boss	---	---	2.54[a,b,c]	2.27
6. Co-Worker	---	---	2.24[a,b]	2.07

*Phase I significantly different from Phase II
[a]Significantly different from Careerists, $p > .05$
[b]Significantly different from Homemakers, $p > .05$
[c]Significantly different from Breadwinners, $p > .05$
[d]1=very likely to disapprove, 5=very likely to approve
[e]1=I am unlikely to do as they wish, 5=I am likely to do as they wish

EMPLOYMENT CONCERNS SINCE COLLEGE

Attraction to Employment

As college students, the Nesters found a career an attractive prospect. Like the Careerists, they wanted and valued having a career, as well as the income it would bring (see Table 6.2). Like the Careerists, in college, the Nesters also confidently believed that if they worked outside the home, they could manage both work and family responsibilities. For instance, if they worked outside the home after childbirth, they thought they would experience variety and a feeling of accomplishment, and be able to maintain their career skills without losing intimacy with their children (see Table 6.3). In spite of their attraction to a career, even in college, they more highly valued the quality of their family relationships than their careers. They especially valued their relationships with their spouses (see Table 6.2).

After undergraduate college, even as better educational and career opportunities expanded the horizons for Careerists and Breadwinners, the Nesters saw their opportunities constrict. Fewer Nesters acquired postgraduate education. For example, about one-third of them went on to do some graduate work compared to half the Careerists. Similarly, half as many Nesters as Careerists received a terminal degree in law or medicine or completed a Ph.D. (see Appendix, Table A.1).

Not having advanced higher education may have constricted the opportunities available to the Nesters. Of course, the alternative could also be true: Perhaps they did not seek advanced education because their families were as important to them as their careers. Graduate education increases longevity in the paid workplace because it provides the opportunity for advanced training, presumably more interesting work, and higher salaries.[1] This lack of advanced higher education may contribute toward Nesters' decision to remain home after childbirth.

A decade after graduating from college, probably in response to restricted opportunities, the Nesters appear less optimistic about what they can accomplish by returning to paid work after childbirth. Compared to when they were students, fewer Nesters associate accomplishment, fun, and variety in their life with employment (see Table 6.3). In many cases they appear "turned off" to their careers. Or, they simply no longer believe the rewards are worth the tradeoffs. As Shelly, a project manager, says:

I ran a department and was expected to set an example by meeting deadlines, no matter what kind of hours. My boss was not organized and so there were always last-minute projects keeping me at work late in the evenings. (Also, he felt men were superior to women.) I spoke to my husband and also to women who did need

Table 6.2
Values of Nesters

Values[d]	Phase I	Phase II
Having fun	4.12	4.38
A sense of accomplishment	4.56	4.56
Feeling tied down	2.00	1.62
Having variety in my life	4.20	4.00
Feeling guilty	1.62	1.44
Feeling resentful	1.50	1.89
Feeling tired	1.44	1.56
Feeling bored	1.50	1.56
Feeling close to my husband	5.00	5.00
Feeling close to my child	4.88	4.73
Running my household smoothly	3.94	4.06
Training my child myself	4.00	4.12
Maintaining my career skills	4.38	4.00
Maintaining my job contacts	4.19	3.81
Advancing my career	4.25	3.75
Earning enough income myself	4.25[b]	3.88
Having enough family income	4.69	4.81
Having extra income	3.94	4.25
Making more $ than it costs me to work	4.06	4.38
Husband needing two jobs	1.56	1.19
Missing child's growth milestones	1.88	1.75
Finding adequate child care	4.27	4.19
Having enough time for the child	4.62	4.69
Having enough time for myself	4.31	4.31
Having enough time for my husband	4.62	4.50
Husband helping around the house	4.38	4.31

Table 6.2 (Continued)

	Phase I	Phase II
Values[d]		
Child will be independent	4.20	4.44
Child will be secure	4.60	4.75
Child will be well disciplined	4.47	4.50
Child will get along easily with others	4.69	4.50
Child will learn beliefs	3.69	---
Child will do better in school	---	4.31
Child will feel loved	5.00	4.88
Child will have attention when needed	4.81[*]	4.56[*]
Child feels closer to others than to me	2.27	2.19
Child will believe women are competent	---	4.56

*Phase I significantly different from Phase II
[a]Significantly different from Careerists, $p > .05$
[b]Significantly different from Homemakers, $p > .05$
[c]Significantly different from Breadwinners, $p > .05$
[d]1=extremely undesirable, 5=extremely desirable

to return to work. They usually expressed a desire to be home with their children—therefore, I feel fortunate to be home with my child. I decided not to work outside my home after childbirth. I considered my job and how much I liked it and how much I might miss work. I concluded that I would not miss it. I decided that I would rather raise my children myself and maybe try to work at home later on.

The Nesters appear to have adopted effective strategies to cope with their decisions not to work outside the home. In their own way, they remain committed to the paid work role, although they no longer engage in paid work and do not see the workplace as very desirable. More Nesters than Breadwinners and Careerists think they can keep their careers going—by maintaining their job contacts and career skills—if they are not employed (compare Table 6.3 with Tables 3.3 and 4.3).

A few Nesters consider starting their own businesses out of their homes in the future. Perhaps they see working at home as a way to earn income while maintaining job contacts and career skills—a way of negotiating paid work–family conflict and eliminating the high psychic cost of working outside the home. Such beliefs may aid their adjustment to the decision to withdraw from paid work.

Table 6.3
Nesters' Perceptions of the Consequences of Working and Not Working Following Childbirth

| | Phase I | | Phase II | |
Consequences[d]	Working	Not Working	Working	Not Working
Having fun	3.93[*]	3.44	3.19[*]	3.75
A sense of accomplishment	4.36[*]	2.88[b]	3.75[*]	3.50
Feeling tied down	2.86	3.62	3.44	3.06
Having variety in my life	4.07[*]	2.62	3.56[*]	3.06
Feeling guilty	2.79	2.69[b,c,*]	3.38	1.88[*]
Feeling resentful	2.23	3.20[b,c]	2.94	2.75
Feeling tired	3.14	3.13[b,c]	4.19	3.06
Feeling bored	2.08	3.69[b,c]	1.69	2.88
Feeling close to my husband	3.71	4.06	3.56	4.00
Feeling close to my child	3.93	4.38	3.69	4.56
Running my household smoothly	3.50[*]	4.06	2.62[*]	4.19
Training my child myself	3.79[b,c]	4.50	2.88	4.81
Maintaining my career skills	4.14	2.56	4.25	2.81[a,c]
Maintaining my job contacts	4.07	2.31	4.19	2.75[a,c]
Advancing my career	3.71	1.88	3.69	1.69
Earning enough income myself	3.86	1.31	3.81	1.44
Having enough family income	4.00	2.93	4.44	3.06
Having extra income	3.93	2.07	4.19	2.19
Making more $ than it costs me to work	4.29	1.47	4.00	2.07
Husband needing two jobs	1.71	2.87[*]	1.62	2.19[*]
Missing child's growth milestones	2.43	2.19	3.31	1.31
Finding adequate child care	3.43	3.50	3.38	2.62
Having enough time for the child	3.86[b]	4.56	2.94	4.38
Having enough time for myself	3.36	4.81	2.56[b]	3.88
Having enough time for my husband	3.86[b]	4.62	2.56	4.25
Husband helping around the house	3.93	2.69	3.87	3.20
Child will be independent	4.00	3.19	3.81	3.56
Child will be secure	3.86	4.06	3.56	4.56
Child will be well disciplined	4.00[b]	3.88[a,c,*]	3.62	4.38[*]

Table 6.3 (Continued)

Consequences[d]	Phase I		Phase II	
	Working	Not Working	Working	Not Working
Child will get along easily with others	4.07	3.62*	3.94	4.25*
Child will learn beliefs	3.50	3.81	---	---
Child will do better in school	3.50	3.94	---	---
Child will feel loved	4.50	4.62	4.12	4.81
Child will have attention when needed	3.79	4.44*	3.69	4.75*
Child feels closer to others than to me	2.57	2.81	2.88	2.19
Child will believe women are competent	4.19	4.12	---	---

*Phase I significantly different from Phase II
[a]Significantly different from Careerists, $p > .05$
[b]Significantly different from Homemakers, $p > .05$
[c]Significantly different from Breadwinners, $p > .05$
[d]1=very unlikely, 5=very likely

Bielby and other researchers report that many college educated women remain committed to the worker role even when they have withdrawn from paid work for childrearing.[2] But remaining committed does not equal remaining effective in maintaining one's career. The Nesters may have unrealistically high expectations of their ability to maintain job skills and contacts while at home with their children, or they may be determined to work harder to maintain such contacts.

Rejecting an Unsupportive Environment

The lack of support Nesters received in their professional lives turns them from paid work to domesticity. Unlike the Careerists and Homemakers, who receive continued support as adults for the life plan they committed themselves to as students, the Nesters faced a generally unsupportive environment. Specifically, more Nesters encountered unsupportive supervisors or co-workers who challenged them to change their career plans (see Table 6.1 and compare to Tables 3.1, 4.1, and 5.1). Also, fewer Nesters than Careerists had on-site child care provided by their companies. In some cases, limited spouse support coincided with limited workplace support, which further facilitated their move toward domesticity. For example, before the birth of her son, Cynthia worked as an editorial assistant at a trade magazine. She left this position because the travel and the pressure were too much for her and because her husband objected to the travel. At the time of her son's birth, she held an editorial position for a consulting firm with only ten employees. When doctors diagnosed her son as neurologically impaired, she requested part-time work. The company would not allow it, so she quit. Cynthia's experience illustrates the cumulative effect such lack of support has on any motivation to remain in the paid labor force after childbirth.

Diminished Career Opportunities

In contrast to Careerists, who experienced rising career aspirations and opportunities, the Nesters have encountered less opportunity for mobility. For example, in terms of career development, more Nesters made a lateral move between their first and second jobs, suggesting fewer rewards or less opportunity in their first, critical job, or perhaps less desire for advancement on their part. Also, more Nesters worked for smaller companies, which traditionally provide fewer benefits, more limited career options, and fewer opportunities to find a mentor (see Appendix, Table A.1). Since more say they would leave their jobs after childbirth if they had no mentor, the fact that they do leave suggests that they have had no one guiding them and fostering their careers (see Appendix, Table A.3).

Yet they do not seem particularly disappointed with some aspects of their actual work. They do not differ from the Careerists in the extent to which they met their expectations about variety, autonomy, stress, amount of travel, etc. They did experience disappointment in their advancement and earnings, however. Fewer Nesters than Breadwinners—the group that unexpectedly returned to work—met their pay and promotion expectations in the jobs they held before childbirth (see Appendix, Table A.2).

Chris, an auditor who started her career working for the federal government, tells us:

If I had it to do all over again, I wouldn't work in the public sector. The salary compression I experienced in my first few jobs out of college had a negative impact on my earnings. It was really discouraging!

In addition, Nesters were particularly disappointed with the lack of leadership they experienced on the job and the lack of role clarity they felt. Such circumstances may contribute to the Nesters' demoralization and reduce their earlier enthusiasm for paid work.

HOME CONCERNS

A desire on the part of many Nesters to feel close to—and presumably win the approval of—a spouse who does not support their career, changed their life plans and moved them out of paid work. They did this also, in part, because they had trouble managing the time demands associated with combining work and family. Although they gave up a career that they found unrewarding, they did not seem to replace it with a commitment to home-making.

Limited Spouse Support

The Nesters' relationships with their spouses most critically turn Nesters toward domesticity. As college students, they anticipated continuing their careers after having a baby. Yet, they valued the quality of their family relationships as much as their careers. Based upon a series of values related to work, family, finances and self, they considered feeling close to their husbands most important. (The group average was 5 on a scale from 1 to 5, indicating that every individual gave this item the highest possible score. See Table 6.2.) They also valued highly feeling close to their children, giving their children enough love and attention, as well as having enough time for their spouses and children. Despite their career intentions, they remained family centered in terms of what they considered important.

In Phase II of the study, the Nesters continue to place heavy emphasis on their personal relationships. In particular, they want to feel close to their husbands most of all; they still all score "5" only on this item, considering it just as important as when they were students.

On the whole, Nesters' partners do not encourage their wives' careers. Compared to the Careerists' partners, fewer Nesters' husbands supported their wives' commitment to their jobs before the birth of their children, and Nester's husbands provide less emotional support for their wives' careers after the births of their children. Nesters and Careerists started out with the same goals, but more Nesters than Careerists became emotionally depend-ent upon a marital relationship with a husband who offered little support for their careers. The risk of losing a close relationship with their husbands presents a strong obstacle to the Nesters' career development. Indeed, if a career can be purchased only at the expense of their marriages, many Nesters prefer to give up aspirations held as college students rather than risk damaging this relationship. The interesting issue, which our data did not address, is why—in contrast to the Careerists—they picked partners who do not support their career intentions.

Over the course of the decade, the Nesters placed increased emphasis on having a good income. They place a high priority on having enough family income and having extra income. In order to meet these income desires if they do not work for pay, they need spouses who are willing and able to become sole breadwinners. They are slightly more likely now to say they will have enough income even if they do not work. And they are significantly less likely now than when they were in college to believe their spouses would need two jobs if they themselves do not work outside the home. Therefore, for many Nesters, their partner's economic, if not career support, enables them to withdraw from the workplace.

There are no objective differences between the groups in spouse's income (see Appendix, Table A.1). Thus, perception of what is adequate or extra income does not necessarily reflect actual income. As with the Homemakers, however, perceptions of adequate income reinforce the traditional division of labor and provide additional justification for Nesters to stay home.

Nesters' choice to put their relationships with their husbands first could start a cycle that is difficult to reverse. Since some have spouses who require complete loyalty to their careers, the Nesters may first sacrifice their own career potential to support the spouse's. In turn, missed career opportunities may lead to unmet pay and promotion expectations. Finally, perception of unmet pay and promotion expectations may serve to reinforce a traditional marital relationship that provides some financial security, and furnishes another reason to stay home.

In summary, long-term commitment to the marital relationship seems to reduce Nesters' attachment to their careers and make domesticity and childrearing more logical options. In some cases, this process is accelerated by mounting frustration with lack of workplace support and career development coupled with their own uncertainty that they can manage two major roles simultaneously.

Time Management Dilemmas

Compared to the would-be Homemakers, in college, the Nesters firmly believed that even if employed, they would have sufficient time for their spouses and children. However, they displayed mixed feelings about the consequences of staying home. On the one hand, they envisioned that staying home would allow more time for the relationships that were so important to them—more time for their children and spouses, and even more time for themselves. On the other hand, unlike the Homemakers, more Nesters believed that not working would result in their feeling guilty, tired, bored, resentful, and less accomplished. Staying home might make them better wives and mothers, but they would suffer some negative consequences (see Table 6.3).

As adults, they perceive that the rewards of the paid workplace do not outweigh the negative consequences to the time management necessary for returning to work after childbirth. The Nesters now believe that working for pay results in the expected income and skill maintenance, but also in fatigue and time conflicts. They do not have enough time for everything they have to do. For example, one woman confides: "I do not feel I am physically or mentally capable of being a wife, mother, businesswoman, and homemaker and doing all four things well."

Even as they stay home to care for their children, many Nesters appear to be overwhelmed and suggest they do not have enough time for themselves. They also are less optimistic than they were as college students that they could run their homes smoothly if they were employed. As one woman, formerly a physical therapist, expresses it, "The increased stress and responsibility of taking care of my son have made it impossible to have any time for myself." The combination of staying home and feeling time-stressed complicates Nesters' mothering.

CHILD CONCERNS

Training Children

Compared to the would-be Homemakers, as students, Nesters firmly believed that, even if employed, they would have sufficient time for their spouses and children, and still be able to discipline and train their children (see Table 6.3). For instance, while more Breadwinners and Homemakers said their children would be well disciplined and sociable if they did not work outside the home, the Nesters believed these outcomes were more likely if they *did work*. In fact, collegiate Nesters—unlike Homemakers—did not view staying home as having a stronger positive impact on their child's socioemotional development (Table 6.3). Instead, they associated working for pay with having a more independent and disciplined child. In some ways, they thought working for pay would make them better mothers.

As adults, they are more likely to believe that not working outside the home will benefit their children's sociability, discipline, and need for attention. While some Nesters, such as Nora in the opening scenario, worry about the impact of day care on their children's development and emotional adjustment, most say that they would return to work if they had adequate child care. Nesters are moderately committed to exclusive maternal care for children (see Appendix, Table A.4).

Changing Child Care Beliefs

Both Nesters and Breadwinners, groups of women who changed their minds about their career/homemaking patterns, worry about day care more than women who persisted in their earlier plans. Thus, Careerists anticipated needing day care and, consistent with their own ideology, believed adequate provisions would be forthcoming to meet their needs. Homemakers, in turn, consistent with their own ideology, wanted to "do it themselves," so they cared less about day care availability. Nesters planned to work outside the home when they were in college, but emphasized their own role as caretaker, planned less carefully for this need, and were more open to seeing day care limitations without perceptions colored by the Careerists' strong beliefs. When faced with the realities of complex schedules and less-than-perfect public and private day care options, they became less confident that either day care workers or they themselves could adequately care for their children.

SELF CONCERNS

Today, the Nesters suffer from the lowest self-esteem ratings of any of the four groups (Appendix, Table A.5), although they say they feel less guilty about staying home now than they thought they would as college students. In part, this low self-esteem seems to arise from inhabiting a homemaker role that is inconsistent with their own desires to have a career and that is also inconsistent with current social norms. In addition, many have suffered from personal crises or tragedies, which made it very difficult to pursue a career and which make them feel out of control.

Adjusting to Domesticity

Nesters do not feel very comfortable as homemakers, as this role does not support their values and self-concepts (Appendix, Table A.4). They do not express the unwavering, almost ideological, commitment of either Careerists or Homemakers. That is, they value commitment to employment less than the Careerists, but they do not value domesticity and childrearing as vigorously as the Homemakers. These responses reflect an ambivalence toward their situation: Nesters appear to make a surface adjustment to domesticity without the clear priorities of the Careerists or the Homemakers. While they may not have very positive feelings about homemaking and domesticity, they also have less positive feelings about the paid workplace. In many ways, withdrawing from paid work for the Nesters appears to be a way of negotiating conflict in their lives.

Meeting Life Crises

In addition to limited spouse support and less than positive experiences in the work force, some Nesters experienced a particular event that advanced the choice of domesticity and childrearing over a career. Such events stand out as important because they altered expectations, recast behavioral patterns, and forced Nesters to reassess and redirect their life courses. Since they personally do not desire this redirection, sometimes Nesters' self-concept is stressed by feelings of lack of control.

For some, geographic mobility triggers recognition that the male partner's career matters more. When conflict over relocation arises, Nesters face moving at the expense of their own careers if they want to maintain their relationships. Charlene, a former systems analyst, describes her situation:

At 30 I have had my first child. In deciding to stay home with my son, I considered attachment to my career versus bonding with the baby. The fact that my husband gets transferred periodically and the toll it has already taken on the progression of my career and attainment of a higher level degree also was important.

For other women, specific events such as a serious health problem—their own or their children's—serve as a catalyst for withdrawing from the work force. Cynthia, a woman with a neurologically impaired son, accounts for her situation:

I'm not planning on working, although I'm concerned about maintaining my career and having enough income. I never really see anything as permanent because of my son's situation. He was born with a developmental disability and it's been very hard for us. Right now, my plans extend about a year into the future. I would like to have another baby, or maybe start my own business, but we're not financially secure enough to take on either right now or in the near future. The most likely alternative for the future is for me to get a part-time job in my field.

A difficult work situation can also trigger withdrawal from paid work. According to Leslie, a systems analyst,

My job required a lot of overtime and bringing work home on weekends. I also had a long commute (two hours on the road each day), so I decided I would not have much time to spend with my child. Five weeks after I gave birth to my daughter we moved across the country to California. I decided that moving, looking for a home, and having a new baby were stressful enough and I didn't need to add looking for a job.

Lost Hopes and Low Confidence

In many cases, Nesters make sensible choices to preserve their marriages and minimize paid work-family conflict. But, for the most part, their choices sacrifice their own personal aspirations. They define a career as something for themselves . . . their own. Feeling selfish about such a "luxury," they willingly sacrifice it for the good of their families. Linda expresses her thoughts on this subject:

Deciding to stay home was a process of taking stock in myself and dealing with my own self-image. After much fretting and anxiety, I realized I was being selfish, being so worried about my accomplishments. I decided to put my skills towards the raising of my child. I then felt proud in choosing, at this stage in life, to put my time and energy into raising this little person. There is time for me in the future.

Feeling guilty and selfish for wanting time for herself and a career and being concerned for her child, Linda interrupted her career.

CONCLUSION

Because so many women in their generation return to work after child-birth, Nesters sometimes encounter disapproval from peers for choosing to stay home. By abandoning their career aspirations for homemaking, they may feel out of step with their generation—choosing domesticity may be as difficult for them as choosing a paid work career was for earlier generations of women. Indeed, their small numbers in this study underscore their isolation. The limited support they receive from significant others—bosses, co-workers, friends and spouses—negative life events, and a pattern of self-sacrifice combine to encourage them to abandon their former career plans and reduce their self-confidence and feelings of well-being.

A number of Nesters mention psychological well-being or physical health in describing their decisions to quit employment after having a child. For instance, one woman says she worries about her "emotional stability" in dealing with feelings of guilt as well as the "emotional stability" of the relationship between her partner and herself. A second acknowledges that therapy helped her decide to stay home. Another woman—who has not yet had a child—feels that "finances and mental health" will influence her decision, and that perhaps group therapy would help her.

On the whole, the Nesters see a career as a luxury or a form of self-cen-teredness. Many take little for themselves—much of their life involves sacrificing for their spouses or children's needs. Yet, they feel ambivalence because they lack a strong belief system that supports commitment to domesticity and family values such as we see with the Homemakers. They do not believe they can care for their children better than others, but they are staying home, nonetheless. On the surface, the Nesters accept the decision to interrupt their careers in favor of stable marriages and secure children. Yet they pay a high price in ambivalence, anxiety, and lack of self-confidence.

NOTES

1. M. H. Strober. (1982). The MBA: Some passport to success for women and men. In P. A. Wallace (Ed.), *Women in the workplace*, pp. 25–44. Boston: Auburn House.

2. D. D. Bielby & W. T. Bielby. (1984). Work commitment, sex role attitudes, and women's employment. *American Sociological Review*, *49*, 234–247; D. D. Bielby & W. T. Bielby. (1988). Women's and men's commitment to paid work and family. In B. A. Gutek, A. H. Stromberg, & L. Larwood (Eds.), *Women and work*, vol. 3, pp. 249–263. Newbury Park, CA: Sage.

Chapter 7

Consistency, Change, and Comparisons

We began this investigation using two theoretical frameworks—life stages and response to social change—to try to answer a few primary questions: When in college, how do women plan to combine work and family roles? What impact do post-collegiate experiences have on women's decisions? What makes some women act consistently with their college plans and others change their minds? What makes some women stay home and others return to work? What implications do these choices have for others? By looking at what we have learned from all four groups, and by comparing our findings to those of other studies, we can begin to answer these questions.

We have selected five studies for comparison. Three are longitudinal studies begun while the women were in college. Two studies are cross-sectional studies of adult women. By comparing results of the study described in this book with these other studies, we can explore not only how young women adapt as their lives develop over time, but how successive generations of college students—influenced by a rapidly changing environment— meet the challenges defined by their generation.

The Radcliffe study first interviewed women from the class of 1964 when they were college seniors.[1] These women matured between the late 1950s and early 1960s era of the feminine mystique and the gathering strength of the 1970s women's movement, which followed their graduation. The Michigan study,[2] initiated in 1967, and followed up in 1971 and 1981, and the Carnegie Mellon study[3] of 1968 examine the lives of college women graduating during peak social turbulence and being thrust out into the maelstrom of changing gender norms and social conditions of the 1970s. Each of these studies examines the transitions in women's lives during a time of national sociopolitical transition and adds additional information to help us interpret what happened to women maturing into adulthood in the 1980s.

We have included two other nonlongitudinal studies to broaden the base of comparison beyond women graduates of selective universities. The *Lifeprints* study is based on interviews with a group of adult women from varying educational and social strata who lived in the Boston area in the late 1970s.[4] The women studied in *Hard Choices* represent similarly diverse backgrounds from the San Francisco area.[5] Both studies were carried out in the late 1970s when the women in our study were still in college. To some extent the women in our study were influenced by the same events as they crafted their initial plans and life choices.

HOW DO COLLEGE WOMEN PLAN TO COMBINE EMPLOYMENT AND FAMILY?

In the ambiguous context of the early 1980s, most college women we contacted had simple plans for employment, childbearing, childrearing, and combining the two roles. Their plans were often not elaborate and did not consider many obstacles or alternatives if they could not accomplish their first goals using their primary strategies. Wide variation and considerable ambivalence make it impossible to generalize accurately, however. Some women had no plans, lived day by day, and preferred it that way. Others had elaborate strategies extending ten or more years into the future and covering lots of contingencies.

Plans for employment typically contained a career goal related to attaining a first position in the occupation of choice and one general strategy for achieving this goal. In some cases it was to get a first job immediately, in others, to continue further education and then gain employment in a preferred field. A few responded with childrearing plans when asked about their careers.

Plans for childbearing typically involved having two to three children beginning in four to five years and spreading them out with two to three years between each childbirth. When asked whether they would change their childbearing or career strategies to combine the two roles, most said they would adjust their family plan rather than change their career plans. Specifically, they would reduce the number of children, delay pregnancy, or spread out their childbearing in order to have the employment they wanted.

Plans for combining childrearing and employment were the most common and elaborate plans. Even women with no other plans had some plan for integrating these two roles in their lives. The most striking characteristic of such plans was their positive expectation that children, husbands, and organizations would cooperate to make this combination work. This optimism did not block anticipation of the need for alternatives, however. Women expected they might have to create elaborate day care strategies or work less than full time or in occupations compatible with child care in order to enact both roles.

HOW DID THEY CHANGE?

The women in all six studies lived through a social transition from a time when domesticity and childrearing were the expected female gender norm to a shift in expectations by 1980, when college was equated with preparing for an employment career. During the 1980s and 1990s the women in our study, as well as the others, enjoyed greater freedom and flexibility in carving out their lifestyle choices. Some remained with their original plans while others modified earlier preferences.

We first questioned the women who participated in this study when they were juniors or seniors in one of two urban, Northeastern state-supported universities. We recontacted them 8–10 years later, asking some of the same questions and also directly asking them how their lives had changed in the interval. We classified women into four categories depending upon how their Phase I and Phase II intentions compared.

As college students, the Careerists intended to work following childbirth and did return to paid employment soon after the birth of their first children. Their identity as professionals reduced ambivalence and supported continuous beliefs that employment was fun and challenging and that spouses and children would benefit rather than suffer from their choices. Spouses, parents, and bosses also supported their choices.

Homemakers linked their identities to providing exclusive maternal care and supporting a family-centered life-style. They were consistent in desiring this life-style as students and adults and reduced their ambivalence by successfully surrounding themselves with spouses, friends, and former co-workers who supported their choices.

Breadwinners expected to stay home after childbirth when they were college students, but returned to paid work as mothers when economic pressures and challenging, well-paid jobs supported a new choice. Because

Breadwinners do not tie their sense of self to either maternal or employee roles, they could choose the most pragmatic option presented by a changing society without jeopardizing their self-esteem. They reduced their ambivalence by recognizing that they enjoyed their paid work, did not like housework very much and contributed needed income to their families.

Finally, Nesters saw themselves as career-oriented as college students, but gave up this dream as adults when they encountered unsupportive employers and husbands or a family member's illness. They pay a high price for this self-sacrifice in shaky self-esteem and continued ambivalence.

How do these changes compare with the changes women reported in the other studies? Women in the Radcliffe study struggled with changing norms in the 1960s. Although a number went to graduate school directly after college, many began with the idea of supporting their husbands and sacrificing their career aspirations. Career-oriented women were considered "pathological" and "selfish." A few years later, they had to face contradictory cultural pressures and not only respond to a "family clock" but to a "career clock" norm as well. The big shift for many was to add an employment career to family responsibilities, usually after their youngest child entered school. By mid-life, those women who remained solely on the family clock immediately after childbirth often returned to paid work after their children left home, but most held lower-status jobs for which they often were overqualified.

The life patterns of Radcliffe women demonstrate some similarities and some differences from the women studied in this book. Like Breadwinners, the Radcliffe women began life believing they would become Homemakers but ended up more like Careerists. However, the Breadwinners' changing life patterns were substantially motivated by the changing economic realities of the 1980s. The women in the Radcliffe study faced pressures that stemmed largely from the 1970s cultural shift in norms for women and the absence of clear and relevant guidelines from the past. Also, they faced these changes later in their lives.

Similar shifts in norms for women propelled the women in the Michigan study. Of these women, three-fourths were employed by the second phase of the study 14 years after graduation; others planned to return at a later date. That number greatly exceeded that predicted by college expectations. Initially, these women were classified either as role innovators (preparing for occupations with 30 percent or less women), as moderates (in occupations of 30 percent to 70 percent women) or as traditionals (in occupations with 70 percent or more women). Between 1967 and 1981, women in occupations defined as moderate were likely to shift to either a role more innovative or a more traditional occupation.

Those women who modified their life scripts and moved into the more innovative occupations found more rewarding, challenging jobs. Much as the Breadwinners became indistinguishable from the Careerists in our study, so some of the University of Michigan moderates came to share the characteristics of the role innovators.

Others in the Michigan study, who became more traditional over time, lowered their career commitment and tended to displace their own achievement needs onto their husbands, in a pattern resembling that of the Nesters. These traditional women also reduced the number of children they wanted. Many of the full-time homemakers—and those who moved to more traditional jobs—became more defensive about the legitimacy of their choices. Perhaps because the women's movement was at its height in the 1970s when many of these women remained committed to childrearing, they felt attacked and devalued. In contrast, the Homemakers in our study were satisfied with their role and their commitment to domesticity. They did not feel the pressure to justify staying home with their children, in part because they found support in a family-values-oriented community.

The women in the Carnegie Mellon study shifted to a more egalitarian household, sharing responsibilities with their spouses regardless of whether or not they were employed. As in our study, more Carnegie Mellon women shifted away from domesticity toward combining paid work and family. Over one-third shifted from a path of full-time homemaking to part-time or full-time employment. In contrast to the Michigan study, however, the graduates of Carnegie Mellon continued to work in women-dominated fields and to prefer working with people rather than things. They remained less interested in high-powered jobs. They adopted a contingency orientation, remaining both fluid and flexible in their strategies, similar to the life plans of the Homemakers.

The women described in *Lifeprints* and *Hard Choices* also learned that marriage and children alone did not guarantee well-being. Indeed, for many, doing and achieving became as important as relationships and feelings. The attitude toward their children that differentiated the employed women from the homemakers in the *Lifeprints* study in many ways resembled the differences between the Careerists and the Breadwinners, on the one hand, and the Homemakers, on the other in this study. In *Lifeprints,* employed women viewed children as rewarding, enjoyed doing things with them, felt proud of them, and liked seeing them mature and change. In contrast, for Homemakers in both studies, children provided a sense of being needed; being the caretaker for a child gave one a sense of being special and irreplaceable.

In *Hard Choices*, among those women who began with domestic orientations, two-thirds developed nondomestic orientations as their lives proceeded. As attachment to the work force grew, they became less interested in domesticity. Once the switch was made from a temporary and tenuous to a permanent and strong labor force commitment, these women were less likely to settle for just any job.

In our study, although more economically driven, Breadwinners' profiles came to resemble those of Careerists, in their enjoyment of work and likelihood of not just settling for any job. But the shift was clearly away from domesticity and housekeeping, not away from interest in their children.

In contrast to the Michigan role-innovators study and the *Hard Choices* study, very few women in our study traded their initial career plans for homemaking. Like the women described in *Hard Choices*, many of the Nesters encountered blocked work opportunities, which enhanced the pull of domesticity. In some cases, these women were in traditional marriages, which insulated them and undermined their career building. Yet even among this group, several planned to return to work when their children were older.

If we look at what *all* of the women have in common, regardless of whether they followed the life pattern of the Careerists, the Breadwinners, the Homemakers, or the Nesters, and if we can determine how their responses and those of the women in other studies differed over time, we can begin to answer the question of how all women change during their twenties.

Tempered Optimism

The most striking feature of all of this study's participants when they were college students was their optimism. Even though there was certainly a range of opinions in the group, in general respondent believed that most aspects of their lives would go well. Their jobs would be challenging and well paid, their homes would be clean, their husbands helpful, and their babies healthy and able to be molded into perfect offspring.

While the world may not have been cold and cruel to those fortunate enough to have obtained a college education, life experiences tempered these opinions to the extent that all of the women hold significantly less optimistic opinions now than they did in college. The difference is not dramatic, in the sense that, on average, all aspects of their lives are now seen as more likely to be good than bad, but youthful extremes are less obvious (see Tables 3.3, 4.3, 5.3, and 6.3).

Now, all women are a little less likely to believe that paid work would bring them a sense of accomplishment, variety, fun, and career advancement. Even though most had worked for pay as college students, the entry- and middle-level jobs they held upon graduation did not live up to some women's dreams of an exciting career. Also, the economic downturn during the 1980s and the beginning of the 1990s influenced whether women were able to advance as rapidly as they expected.

When thinking about their home lives as adults, all women are more likely now than as college students to believe they would feel tied down, resentful, or tired if they stay home after they become mothers. They are also less likely to believe they would be able to run their households smoothly if they were full-time homemakers than they had thought as students.

In some of the earlier studies such as the Radcliffe study, those women who had chosen to combine roles—on both the career and the family clock—felt the strain of juggling multiple roles and going against societal norms at the same time. Although women in all studies grew with the times, they did not have the perfectly ordered lives some may have anticipated in college. The greater complexity and choices that confronted each successive group tempered the optimism many felt as college students. In all studies, most women gained a strengthened sense of self and competence but became increasingly realistic as well.

One wonders if their college perceptions of the ease of homemaking reflected the relatively low value placed on this role when they were growing up during the beginning of the women's liberation era of the 1970s. A set of popular ideas might have supported this view. "If women do it, it can't be too hard." "The men's world of paid work is much more challenging and difficult and requires strength and skill." "Women can be just as strong and skillful as men, and we will prove it in the paid *workplace*, not the *home place*." These ideas filled the rhetoric of the day. Perhaps, with so many women in the labor force during the 1990s, it has become more difficult and lonely to manage a household without a neighbor or mother or grandmother or aunt to give advice, help, or baby sit when needed, because these women also are working outside the home.

Difficulties in Time Management

In general, as college students, all of the women believed it would be easier to have enough time to do all of the things they wanted to do than they report as adults. While all share the concern that there are not enough hours in the day, what they would do with more time differs by study and by group.

Careerists as college students underestimated how much time and attention husbands and children would need. More Careerists now value having enough time to care for their children, and fewer believe they would have enough time and energy to train their children, make them feel loved and give them enough attention, if they work for pay. Also, fewer now believe that they will have enough time for their husbands if they stay home after childbirth.

Both Breadwinners and Homemakers are less likely to believe they would have enough time for themselves if they stayed home after childbirth than they thought during college. Like the Careerists, in college, they thought they would have more time if they stayed home than they do now, but Breadwinners and Homemakers now say they, themselves, are the losers, not their husbands and children.

All groups also seem to hold beliefs that confirm their current life choices. Homemakers are now less likely to believe they would be able to run a smooth household, train their children, and give them needed attention if they had chosen to work; Breadwinners and Careerists are more likely to believe they would have the time and opportunity to train their children if they worked than they had thought as students.

Nesters are out of time altogether as adults. Fewer now believe they would have enough time for their children and their husbands if they worked. But they also are somewhat less likely to believe they would have enough time for their husbands, children, and self if they do not work, the actual choice they made.

Regardless of which path they selected, the women in all studies encountered difficulties in time management on a day-to-day basis as well as in the long term. For instance, in the Radcliffe study, many women who combined paid work and family acknowledged they always felt they were playing catch-up. This chronic feeling of having too much to do spilled over into long-term career plans as well. Some women planned to return to graduate school or pursue full-time careers but the time was never right.

Another issue that appears in all six studies is that women perceive difficulties in time management both as a result of too many roles and due to dissatisfaction with not having enough time for each role. All women experienced some level of conflict and strain. In the Michigan study, levels of reported role conflict rose from one-fifth of subjects shortly after graduation from college to half the women fourteen years later. The role innovators experienced less conflict than women in traditional careers. In the Carnegie Mellon study, women who juggled multiple roles were physically and psychologically healthier at mid-life. Yet even women who were content to take care of their families were dissatisfied with time management. In several of the studies, family-oriented women were more likely to feel they never had enough time to finish everything. The Nesters, whose lives turned out differently from the way they anticipated in college, also never seemed to have enough time and often felt stressed.

Three factors facilitated effective time management strategies in several studies. First, women with multiple roles were able to settle for less than perfect standards. Like Homemakers, women employed full time see their children as their priority. But they accept that they are not perfect mothers and cannot be all things to all people. For instance, one woman in the Carnegie Mellon study acknowledged that at times her children went to school in ripped clothes.

Second, employment sometimes facilitated management of multiple time demands. In the *Lifeprints* study, for example, many employed women noted that having a full-time job enabled them to say no to tasks, doing favors, and volunteer work that they would have felt compelled to do as homemakers.

The third factor that facilitated effective time management was a supportive spouse. Many of the more career-oriented women in our study married men who supported their ambitions. In *Hard Choices*, work-oriented women had spouses who played a critical role. These men offered emotional support and/or instrumental support such as helping around the house. Similarly, in the *Lifeprints* study, having caring husbands was related to wives' pleasure and happiness.

Shifts in the Importance of Employment and Children

All participants in this study made one shift more strongly related to their stage of life than to the historical era: The value of their employment careers declined while the value of their children remained high (see Tables 3.2, 4.2, 5.2 and 6.2). The most dramatic change occurred among the Careerists, who had valued the career part of their lives so highly as students.

In the midst of their childbearing years, not surprisingly they think a lot about children. However, it is not clear if they decreased their career importance because their own attention has shifted or because they have discovered that career opportunities for women in the 1990s are not all they are cracked up to be.

WHAT INCREASED CONSISTENCY BETWEEN COLLEGE AND ADULTHOOD?

During the end of the teen years and the beginning of their twenties, most young adults make major life choices such as what college major to select, what job to select upon graduation, and whom to choose as a significant-other relationship. In all of these choices, most young adults and others who are affected by their choices hope that early intentions will persist and provide the basis for their actions as life progresses. In some cases, this is true, in others, it is not.

If we look at what the Careerists and Homemakers (who acted on their earlier plans) have in common, and if we can identify how they differ from the Nesters and Breadwinners (who changed their minds), we can understand some of the dynamics that promote consistency between youth and adulthood.

Planning Specificity

Some parents, counselors, and young adults believe that planning may reduce ambiguity and ambivalence and improve the consistency between early and later adulthood. In a culture that values rationality, goal direction, and achievement, people often credit planning with being the means by which all of these things may be gained. Since we asked college students to describe their plans for working, for childrearing, and for combining work and childrearing, we can explore just how planning did or did not contribute to consistency between intentions and actions.

If we look at just the measures of overall planning, Careerists and Homemakers, who were more consistent, did not do more general planning than Breadwinners and Nesters, who were not consistent. If we look more closely, however, we see that consistency does not rest on the sheer amount of planning, but on the kind of planning done (see Table 7.1).

Those who more consistently act on past plans make more detailed plans with more steps or subgoals they intend to accomplish in pursuit of their long-term goals, as well as more alternative plans to consider if somebody blocks their preferred route to their goal. More detailed steps and alternatives occurred whether the long-term goal was one of career accomplishment for Careerists or of childrearing for the Homemakers. Careerists had the most detailed plans of any group and, in particular, had the largest number of alternative career plans. They seemed to think planning was important to be able to accomplish home and work goals simultaneously.

We cannot determine from our information whether the process of creating detailed plans led to more realistic expectations or whether those who had more realistic expectations saw the need for making detailed alternative plans However, there is a relationship. For example, among those now employed, the planners more than the nonplanners realized as college students that employed motherhood would be tiring and that choosing to stay home might lead to loss of career skills. Likewise, among Homemakers and Nesters, those who planned more rather than those who planned less saw, as college students, that they might lose their career skills if they stayed home.

Table 7.1

College Plans for Employment and Childbearing

	Careerists	Homemakers	Breadwinners	Nesters
	%	%	%	%
1. Career Goals*				
None	1.3	---	1.4	6.3
General	57.3	83.6	72.9	43.8
Specific	41.3	16.4	25.7	50.0
2. Career Strategies*				
None	9.5	12.8	3.3	6.3
General	68.9	74.5	81.4	81.3
Specific	21.6	12.7	14.3	12.5
3. Career Blocks				
0	61.3	65.5	64.3	56.3
1	25.3	30.9	25.7	37.5
2	12.0	1.8	7.1	6.3
3	1.3	1.8	2.9	---
4. Career Alternatives				
0	60.0	76.4	72.9	62.5
1	26.7	20.0	18.6	31.3
2	9.3	1.8	5.7	---
3	2.7	---	1.4	6.3
4	1.3	1.8	1.4	---
5. Career Plan Length*				
1 day at a time	12.0	20.0	14.3	37.5
1 year	12.0	9.1	15.7	12.5
2-5 years	42.7	49.1	44.3	37.5
6-10 years	17.3	14.5	17.1	---
More than 10 years	16.0	7.3	8.6	12.5

Table 7.1 (Continued)

	Careerists	Homemakers	Breadwinners	Nesters
	%	%	%	%
6. Plans to Combine Work				
and childbearing				
None	12.0	13.0	14.1	18.8
General	72.0	67.9	70.4	56.3
Specific	16.0	15.1	15.5	25.0
7. Combining Plan Length				
1 day at a time	---	---	---	---
1 year	90.7	92.5	93.8	85.9
2-5 years	2.7	1.9	6.3	1.4
6-10 years	4.0	1.9	---	2.8
More than 10 years	2.6	3.8	---	8.0

*Groups are significantly different, $p \geq .05$

If we look at all of the differences in perceptions between college and later, those who had detailed plans changed their beliefs less and had their job expectations met or exceeded more often than those who planned less. They seemed less stricken by the unrealistic optimism mentioned earlier.

In the three longitudinal comparison studies, planning was limited. To the extent that women did construct plans in college, such plans were frequently mitigated by changing social, economic, and personal conditions. Even when career plans were made, they often were modified or limited by social pressures as well as major family commitments. In the Radcliffe study, 50 of the women went directly to graduate school, yet their early marriages and childbearing suggest limited career planning. Women solely on the career clock had the most difficulty adjusting initially. For others, early involvement with their families compromised career plans and possibilities, and many never really developed their careers even after their children were grown.

Although many women didn't plan, the more career-oriented women reported higher levels of planning than less career-oriented women. The most career-oriented women in college—the role innovators in the Michigan study and the Careerists in our study—reported that their own careers were more important as seniors, they were more likely to plan to obtain higher degrees, and they asserted their intentions to boyfriends and spouses. Early graduate training helped consolidate career plans. For example, in the Michigan study, career-oriented role innovators were more likely to post-pone childbearing and eventually had fewer children.

For many women, plans changed even while in college. In the Carnegie Mellon study, virtually all the women wanted to marry and have children but varied as to how much paid work they planned to incorporate in their lives. During their four undergraduate years, some women increased their plans for employment while other decreased these plans. Changes in life-style and occupational plans were common. Even among the most family-oriented women, the issue of an employment career was always on the table. Many women considered a career as backup: necessary in the event that something happened to their husband or if he could not support the family. Because they were backup plans, they often were less specific. One outcome of having less firm career plans and being uncertain of a preferred job choice was that these young women wavered in the face of obstacles and expressed doubt, which in turn, resulted in being less steadfast about career goals.

Beliefs and Values Congruence

Detailed planning was not the only factor that differentiated those who were consistent from those who were not consistent with their college plans. The former placed a high value on their chosen path and saw it as more fun, varied, and guilt-free than the alternative. During the time of rapidly changing gender role ideologies and increasingly turbulent social change, no particular pattern was the most satisfying. This comment from the Michigan role-innovators study also describes our study ten to fifteen years later: "It didn't matter which path she walked; what mattered was the sense she made of it."

The Careerists and the Homemakers had the strongest, most consistent belief and value systems even though the content of those systems differed. Each group expressed life satisfaction: The Careerists valued their career skills and achievement while Homemakers highly valued adequate child care and observing and assisting child development. Those who changed their minds during the 1980s had intermediate values for consequences of both alternatives: Breadwinners saw both a continuous career and home-making as moderately appealing, the Nesters found neither alternative very attractive (see Tables 3.2, 4.2, 5.2 and 6.2). This moderation could have made it easier to change their minds in an ambiguous environment because they listened more openly to the strong opinions of others who were important to them. Change also may cost less because they have less to lose in public commitment to one or the other life plan than those more highly, and perhaps more openly, committed to one or the other alternative.

The Radcliffe respondents and the role innovators in the Michigan study with the most career-oriented value system tended not to marry or married later and had smaller families, indicating some consistency between values and a variety of behaviors. But most women in the earlier studies shifted toward paid work values only as adults, after changing external realities enabled them to express (and act on) these preferences. As one woman in the *Lifeprints* study noted, "Women have to make choices. They no longer have a duty just to be there."

Environmental Support

Most people believe that individuals do not do as they plan or intend to earlier because something in the environment must have changed or prevented them from doing so. To some extent this was true. A few potential Careerists ended up unemployed or with an illness in the family that required home care, and a few potential Homemakers were unable to have children. But this happened to a much smaller degree than one might expect. Those who changed their minds to continue working were *not* primarily those unable to have children, and those who changed their minds about working were *not* usually unable to find employment. The much more common and more subtle environmental effect was one of social support rather than physical constraint.

Those who were more consistent received steady social support for their choices. More Careerists had working mothers and parents and spouses and bosses who approved of their choices. More Homemakers had nonworking mothers and parental and spouse support for becoming full-time mothers (see Tables 3.1, 4.1, 5.1, and 6.1). Like the Homemakers, many women depicted in *Hard Choices* also married men who were less likely to approve of women working outside the home and supported a preference for homemaking and child care. But similar to the women in the Carnegie Mellon study, there was a trend toward greater egalitarianism in the distribution of household tasks and child care. On the whole, the Homemakers in our study were very comfortable with their beliefs and appear less conflicted and defensive about their life-style preferences than women in the other studies who chose similar paths during the height of the women's movement. Women in *Hard Choices* were "threatened with erosion of structural and ideological supports for domesticity and they struggled to support choices that could have been taken for granted just a short time earlier" (p. 132).

In contrast, those who changed their minds got social support for their change—more Breadwinners who originally expected to stay home found husbands and bosses who encouraged them to work; more Nesters found unsupportive work environments and spouses who did not support their careers emotionally or through their own career choices. Breadwinners responded to general societal environmental change, while Nesters responded more to specific changes in their own life events. In both cases, responsiveness to environmental change depended upon women not linking their identities to either the role of mother or the role of paid worker.

General social support shifted during the time of the comparison studies. Chronologically, the first comparison study began with women who graduated in 1964, prior to the onset of this transitional period. Many of these women already had made significant family commitments and played down their employment careers. The next two studies occur during the height of the women's movement, the civil rights struggle, assassinations, and all the social turbulence of the late 1960s and early 1970s. Many of these historical, institutional, and personal pressures continued to shift during the 1970s. Members of these studies attributed the support of the women's movement, in particular, with raised self-esteem, which in turn enabled them to consider possibilities that had seemed remote just a few years earlier. What is clear is that while the fundamental choices were the same, the costs and benefits associated with each alternative had begun to shift.

The women in this study, chronologically last in the group, had grown up watching their mothers struggle with these issues. By the time they entered college, combining paid work and family was common. The rapidly changing environment resulted in new issues to consider when negotiating work and family choices. Just a decade or so earlier, women felt greedy or self-centered if they wished to work outside the home. Now, women are concerned about making economic sacrifices to *not* work outside the home. Dramatically increased cost of living, corporate downsizing, and technology that made telecommuting a realistic option have emerged as new issues. These environmental realities had less impact on the lives of women in earlier studies.

WHAT INFLUENCES WOMEN TO RETURN TO WORK SOON AFTER BIRTH?

When we look at each group of women, the paths they have chosen seem so different that it is difficult to see what the Breadwinners and Careerists have in common that differentiates them from the Nesters and Homemakers, who chose to leave their work for a more extended time after childbirth. A few commonalities exist, however.

Facilitators of Employed Mothers

Those who return to paid work in less than three years after the birth of their first child (in fact, often in less than one year) primarily found that their prechildbirth jobs were very rewarding in terms of financial gain and challenge. They would have liked to have been rewarded with advancement as well, but they experienced less advancement than they expected.

In the domestic sphere, Careerists and Breadwinners do not like homemaking and childrearing as much as the other groups. Even though they think their children's welfare is extremely important, they believe good child care can be carried out by either mothers or others. In fact, they often believe that their children can benefit from having a happy, active, challenged mother and from social interaction with another caregiver or other children.

Those who returned to work quickly have social support for the role of working motherhood. They chose husbands and jobs to support their own preference. As a result, their husbands support it, their bosses and co-workers support it, and either their parents approve of it or the women are increasingly willing to go against their parents' approval to do what they believe is best for themselves.

In each study, employed mothers had strong feelings of self-efficacy and competence, and most enjoyed high levels of satisfaction in their lives. Most employed mothers desired to maintain balance in their lives. While they were interested in demonstrating competence in their careers, they valued caring for their families. They expressed less interest in domesticity than stay-at-home mothers, but were no less attached to or interested in their children's welfare and development. Despite continuous paid employment and the prominence of work in their lives, it is uncommon to see a desire for all-out achievement in the women of any study similar to that noted among men of comparable ages by developmental theorists such as Levinson.[6]

Support of Stay-at-Home Mothers

In contrast, those who have chosen to stay home with their infants, at least until the children enter school, value domesticity and believe they are good primary caretakers. In particular, Homemakers believe no one else can provide loving, consistent discipline as well as they can. They share this belief with those close to them—their husbands, their bosses, their friends, and their parents. Nesters were both less self-confident that they could do a good job and equally pessimistic about day care.

In most cases, their mothers chose not to work when the women were children and, in general, they find this life pattern worthy of emulating. This is not to say that they find their choice an easy one, however. Both the Nesters and the Homemakers find staying home tougher than they expected, but Homemakers saw it as so positive as college students that it would have been hard not to find it more difficult than expected. Because Homemakers' choices reflect their identification with themselves as mothers, they are happy and self-confident about their choice. Nesters have no such identification with the role of homemaker and, therefore, pay a higher price in lower self-esteem.

In contrast to earlier studies when women had to justify staying at home during the women's movement, the Homemakers in our study felt perfectly comfortable with their life-style choices. Yet as *Hard Choices* reveals, many women exchanged allegiance to their partner's career for emotional and financial support.

As with employed mothers, there were differences among the stay-at-home mothers. Many had made this commitment based on values developed early in their lives. All is subordinated to reproduce a life-style supported by traditional values and ideology: The child suffers when the mother is not in the home. Others, such as the Nesters in our study, came to this realization partly from blocked career aspirations. Disappointed by unmet career aspirations, they considered other options as an outlet for meaningful work. For many, domesticity became that option.

In conclusion, we find that consistency between plans and actions arises from strong self-knowledge of personal preferences and detailed contingency planning. Women who work outside the home after becoming mothers have a personal career commitment, jobs with high financial and challenge rewards, and supportive supervisors, husbands, and friends. On the other hand women who decide to stay home with a baby believe strongly that they are the best caretakers for their babies, have husbands who support them in this choice, and have had work experiences that were unrewarding or unsupportive of their continued employment.

We began Chapter 1 with a description of life stage and sociohistorical explanations for developmental changes in young adulthood. As we look back across the lives of the women in this study, we find helpful insights from both perspectives.

Careerists, Homemakers, and Breadwinners demonstrate different, effective solutions to the developmental tasks of forging an identity based on choosing a way to begin a family and become a competent adult contributor to the society.

Even though the adult roles vary from employed professional and breadwinner to homemaker, members of each of these groups have solved the challenge of young adulthood in ways that boost their self-esteem and gain social approval from those close to them. Nesters, who linked their identity to becoming professionals as they entered young adulthood, but do not see themselves as very effective caretakers even though they chose this role as mothers, have been less successful in solving the developmental tasks of this life stage. They reflect this ongoing problem when they question their own competence.

Careerists provide some support for an age- and stage-related transition of re-evaluation around age thirty. They reshuffled maternal and professional role priority during their late 20s and early 30s. Breadwinners most reflect the effects of sociohistorical change on their developmental course. Since their identities were not tightly linked in adolescence to either maternal or professional roles, they did not selectively choose employment or spouses to support a particular ideology-based women's role. As the society adopted new gender role norms and economic realities, Breadwinners responded to the new-found opportunities and social support.

In one sense, these results are not surprising. However, some implications of these findings are inconsistent with what women and organizations currently do. In the next chapter, we explore these implications in more detail.

NOTES

1. A. J. Stewart & E. A. Vandewater. (1994). The Radcliffe class of 1964: Career and family social clock projects in a transitional cohort. In K. D. Hulbert & D. T. Schuster (Eds.), *Women's lives through time*, 234–258. San Francisco: Jossey Bass; A. J. Stewart & J. M. Healy. (1989). Linking individual development and social changes. *American Psychologist, 44*, 30–42; A. J. Stewart. (1978). A longitudinal study of coping styles of self-defining and socially defined women. *Journal of Consulting and Clinical Psychology, 46*, 1079–1084; A. J. Stewart & P. Salt. (1981). Life stress, life styles, depression and illness in adult women. *Journal of Personality and Social Psychology, 40*, 1063–1069.

2. S. S. Tangri & S. R. Jenkins. (1994). The University of Michigan class of 1967: The women's life paths study. In K. D. Hulbert & D. T. Schuster (Eds.), *Women's lives through time*, 259–281. San Francisco: Jossey Bass; S. S. Tangri. (1972). Determinants of occupational role-innovation among college women.

Journal of Social Issues, *28*, 177–200; S. S. Tangri & S. R. Jenkins. (1986). Stability and change in role innovation and life plans. *Sex Roles*, *13*, 647–662; S. R. Jenkins. (1987). Need for achievement and women's careers over 14 years: Evidence for occupational structure effects. *Journal of Personality and Social Psychology*, *53*, 922–932.

3. S. S. Angrist & E. M. Almquist. (1994). The Carnegie Mellon class of 1968: Families, careers, and contingencies. In K. D. Hulbert & D. T. Schuster (Eds.), *Women's lives through time*, 282–302. San Francisco: Jossey Bass; S. S. Angrist & E. M. Almquist. (1975). *Careers and contingencies*. New York: Dunellen; E. M. Almquist & S. S. Angrist. (1970). Career salience and atypicality of occupational choice among college women. *Journal of Marriage and the Family*, *32*, 242–249; E. M. Almquist, S. S. Angrist, & R. Mickelson. (1980). Women's career aspirations and achievements: College and seven years after. *Sociology of Work and Occupations*, *7*, 367–384.

4. G. Baruch, R. Barnett & C. Rivers. (1983). *Lifeprints: New patterns of love and work for today's women*. New York: Signet.

5. L. Gerson. (1985). *Hard choices*. Berkeley: University of California.

6. D. J. Levinson, C. N. Darrow, E. B. Klein, M. Levinson, & B. McKee. (1978). *The seasons of a man's life*. New York: Knopf.

Chapter 8

Implications and Future Directions

This study has something important to say to women wanting to understand their options and to the organizations that employ them. For women and the career counselors who may help them make important decisions about their lives, we can look at what reduces ambivalence, contributes to consistency, and meets expectations, as well as what contributes to the flexibility to adjust to changing times. For managers of human resources and strategic planning in organizations, we can examine what employment practices contribute to competitive advantage by offering attractive jobs, reducing unwanted turnover, and encouraging valued employees to return to work quickly after childbirth. For all, we can raise the issues yet to be solved and look at future challenges.

THE IMPLICATIONS FOR INDIVIDUAL PLANNING AND CAREER COUNSELING

Although young women thinking about their futures may wonder, "Which is the better choice?" or "What should I prepare to do?" or "What will be good for my children?," the primary message of this book is that there is no one easy answer to these questions. Certainly, it seems clear from these findings that it is possible to have a life that is rewarding and valued with either alternative.

Know Your Own Values

One of the most important implications of our findings is to focus on the most productive questions. It is not "What *should* I do?" but "What do I *like* to do?" Once that is answered, then one can ask, "What is it really like to have a career and work in a large or small organization?" "What is it really like to be a homemaker and take care of children and a husband and an apartment or house?" Then you can ask, "Which of these alternatives is most similar to what I like to do?" And finally you can ask, "How can I do what I like to do in a way that will be good for me, my husband, and my children?"

While this sounds simple and self-evident, the question of "What do I prefer and value" is at the heart of adolescent struggles for identity and continues to be a central life focus of introspective individuals throughout adulthood. The reason this question, so simple to pose and so difficult to answer, is the key question is that it plays a crucial role in encouraging consistency between early and later adulthood and in promoting satisfaction with life choices if a woman decides to change her mind.

Traditional conceptualizations of career counseling often address "knowing yourself" and "knowing the occupation" as keys to successful and satisfying life choices. The life stories told in this book certainly reinforce these ideas as being important. But the central idea of these findings is more specific than just "know yourself"—it is "identify what you like as the first step" in reducing ambivalence about life choices.

Seeing this as a key issue also highlights an important role for those who work to help and support women as they make important life choices. One of the most important things a counselor, teacher, parent, friend, or spouse can do is to work again and again on "values clarification," or the process of identifying what a person really wants and values. Many books[1] of formal exercises and instruments are available in local libraries that women themselves, as well as professionals and family members, can use to explore personal values and preferences and to tie these values into life planning.

In addition to formal techniques of values clarification, these findings also remind us that it is important to affirm the unique preferences of each woman as she matures and to give her the self-confidence to learn to become self-affirming as she makes her life choices. In the political frenzy of affirming "family values," some media may conceptualize this choice as "either family or self." It may be seen as "unladylike" or even immoral for a woman to put her own needs and preferences "ahead of" the needs, wishes, and preferences of her family (especially her children). In order to clarify that choosing a professional career may not be an "antifamily" or an "antichild" choice, we need to explore the impact of life choices on children.

Assess Realistic Consequences for Children

The diversity of life choices made by the women in this book serves as a reminder that it is not an absolute choice to do either what's good for mothers or what's good for children. Most of the women in this book believe they are making choices that are in the best interests both of their children and of themselves, and a growing body of evidence suggests that they are probably right.

In the book *Employed Mothers and Their Children*,[2] a review of factors that promote child welfare makes it clear that maternal employment *per se* is not the crucial factor in deciding what is good for children. Individual characteristics of the child and the family that exist prior to employment seem to play a more important role than employment itself. And the most consistent empirically supported findings are that children of mothers who are satisfied and not feeling guilty about the role choices they have made, and children of mothers whose family members support their choices, have the most positive outcomes for social, intellectual, and emotional development. That is, children of mothers who are living satisfying lives benefit; and women who are doing what they like to do, in the context of others who think they are doing the right thing, are more satisfied with their lives.

The women in this book who are doing what they really want to do are doing what is best for their children, whether they have chosen to be at home or at the office. The Careerists and Breadwinners believe their children will benefit from their mothers' life choices by becoming more independent and sociable as they spend time in a day care setting with other children. Evidence about the effects on children of placement in good day care centers affirms this belief. Homemakers, in turn, believe it is difficult to get child care that will be consistent in discipline and will teach their own values better than they can do this themselves. Numerous articles in the popular press promoting the need for more high-quality, affordable day care facilities support these beliefs.

Seen in this light, the choice might be rephrased as follows: "Do I prefer to spend my time seeking high-quality child care and preparing for and working in a career that enables me to afford to pay for this child care?" or "Do I prefer to provide this kind of child care myself?" When the choice is phrased in this way, it is possible to select a life pattern that is good for a child and that suits the mother's personal values and preferences.[3]

Assess Realistic Consequences for Women

Even though knowing personal preferences and values is the key first step, that step alone is not enough to reduce ambivalence about life choices in an ambiguous, changing environment. Evidence from this study suggests that many young women do not have an accurate picture of what employment and homemaking are like. Therefore, a second step to making life pattern choices is providing or seeking out settings where women can develop realistic expectations about a range of possibilities on the job and at home.

Evidence from the women in this book suggests some common characteristics of each pattern. If we look at the consequences and implications of each choice, we might help women develop a more accurate picture of these alternatives.

Key characteristics that identified Careerists are their consistent desire to remain in the workplace, their continued pursuit of higher education, their dislike of house work, and their development of positive relationships with supportive husbands, bosses, and co-workers. Life experiences between Phase I and Phase II taught them that employment was not quite as ideal or high paying, husbands were not quite as helpful, and children were a little more interesting than they had expected. But these experiences did not change their beliefs enough to make their choice *less* valuable than home-making.

There are implications for work life, home life, and personal life that women might learn from these stories. If a woman decides, while she is still in school, that she wants a continuous employment career, she increases her opportunities to pursue further education helpful to this career. She may also include this desire in her thinking when evaluating potential job opportunities and potential spouses, thereby increasing the social support available for her choice.

A Careerist's clear sense of priorities also focuses her efforts on finding good child care and reduces the stress of feeling guilty about not doing what is best for her child and of chronically wanting to be in two places at once after her children are born. The combination of knowing what she desires and planning well enough to be successful in getting what she wants has a positive effect on her feelings of self-confidence about the future as well.

The most negative implication of this life pattern choice is that if a woman's identity is heavily tied to a particular definition of a career as "upward mobility in a large corporation," economic and organizational constraints make achieving this goal difficult. Disappointments may challenge women to redefine career success and to disentangle their self-concepts from one so closely tied to the upward mobility process.

As we have seen, Homemakers commit to domesticity just as consistently as the Careerists commit to careers in paid employment. Homemakers see their primary role as family caretakers and believe this will prove best for their children. Their experiences since becoming mothers have taught them that homemaking leaves less time for themselves than they thought and reduces future job options more than they expected.

The implications of this choice depend a great deal on the future of the family unit. Knowing that job choices are not going to be a lifetime commitment, a woman who chooses a Homemaker life pattern is free to take a wider variety of jobs if she expects her early employment to be short term. She may be free to choose a job based on whether or not the tasks are appealing or the job is readily available, without having to consider its long-term career potential. If the family proves stable and the spouse is a good economic provider, the freedom to leave an undesirable paid job and the satisfaction of performing the desirable work of homemaking may be the most positive outcomes of this life pattern. The opportunity to provide individualized, consistent child care, valued and enjoyed by women who choose this life pattern, can be an affirming experience for mother and child. While the husbands benefit by having fewer household responsibilities, they pay a price in working longer hours on the job. They also pay a price in lower *family* incomes, even though the *husbands'* incomes average those of all other groups.

If the family is less stable, however, a woman who has chosen to become a homemaker may not be well prepared to assume the role of economic provider should the need arise.[4] Even if the family is stable, women who make this choice will have to redefine their roles and their self-concepts as their children mature and leave home. While some expect this change if they see homemaking as one life stage to be followed by a paid work career later, others who have defined themselves solely as Homemakers may face a more difficult transition in identity development as well as in career development.

The Breadwinners had college profiles similar to Homemakers, and Phase II profiles similar to Careerists, but they expressed moderation in their beliefs at both times. These women grew more independent from the expectations of their parents and more flexible in responding to the social and economic changes as they occurred. When they discovered that work was more fun and financially rewarding than they expected, and homemaking less rewarding than they expected, they were able to change their plans and adapt to new circumstances.

The implications of this life pattern choice are a mirror image of the implications outlined for the Homemakers. Because they were not particularly career oriented in college, fewer Breadwinners attained further higher education and had high expectations of the world of paid work. Their lower career ambitions made satisfaction with early jobs more likely. Lack of further education may mean that their wages will eventually fall behind those of the Careerists. To maintain their future income, Breakwinners may need to return to school at a higher cost in lost wages later in their lives. By remaining in the workforce, however, they avoid one of the most difficult consequences of the Homemaker choice, being unable to assume financial responsibilities if their family structures require it. In an era when less than 25 percent of all families contain children and two parents, this is an important consideration often neglected by college students, but valued by Breadwinners, as they changed their plans to fit their new perceptions of reality.

The Nesters, in turn, believed they wanted to have a continuous career in college but became homemakers after childbirth. This small group changed in a way that was contrary to the larger social changes occurring around them, but responsive to the circumstances of their individual lives. They seemed to change their plans not out of independence or rebellion, but out of concern for the wishes of their spouses and supervisors, or in response to family needs.

The implications of this life pattern are contradictory and perpetuate ambivalence. On the one hand, this choice gave these women the spousal support important to them. In a few cases, the decision to give up their own jobs to move with a husband or to care for a sick child or their own health provided a sense of purpose to their lives. The stories of these women also provide a reminder that a life plan etched in stone may not always lead to the desired goal and that all futures cannot be anticipated.

The other implications of the Nester life pattern seem less positive. While we do not know from evidence in this study whether this life pattern *caused* this finding, we do know that the Nesters, on average, were less self-confident, more ambivalent about their choices, and less satisfied with their experiences at home and at work. A person who believes she wants a career and later considers changing her mind may want to think carefully about how she can make this change in her life plans and also maintain a strong sense of self.

If these are the implications of each life pattern, how can we make them clear to those in the process of making life choices? Children observe their own families' and their relatives' careers, and many young women reported this as an important arena where their initial impressions developed. But childhood observations alone do not generate an accurate picture of what a different home or office life might be, or even what this home or office life is really like for the adults in their own families. One danger of focusing exclusively on protecting our children is that we sometimes overprotect them and keep them from seeing unpleasant or boring aspects of home and employment roles that they need to know about to make informed decisions about their own lives. The adult question is, "How can we provide or seek out these opportunities to learn what we need to know if we attained an incomplete picture as a child, or if the information we learned as a child no longer is relevant to a changing world?"

For the women in this study, practical experiences in baby sitting and other forms of teen employment relate to more realistic and more consistent choices to become Homemakers or Careerists. Encouraging such experiences may, therefore, be one mechanism for providing young women with a more realistic picture of the future. For women who have passed these youthful experiences, other strategies such as seeking out role models and opportunities for discussions with older women about their lives might assist this process. Community programs such as OPTIONS or WOMEN IN TRANSITION found in Philadelphia provide settings where discussions with other women offer opportunities to learn about possible consequences of alternative life patterns.

Make Detailed Career Plans

When it comes down to actually making specific plans for specific life choices in a changing, ambiguous environment, the crucial factor is *detail*. General pictures of preferring homemaking or employment roles did not support either flexibility or consistency between early and later adult choices for the women in this study. Rather, consistency in the life patterns of Homemakers and Careerists is related to having a *detailed* picture of the steps needed to reach a desired goal and alternatives to use if the preferred routes are not readily available. About one fourth of all of the women had made such detailed plans, and these women were the most likely to live out the plans they made.

When we consider the implications of what happened to those who had less detailed planning, we may decide either that we should promote more detailed career planning earlier in women's lives so that they can adequately prepare themselves for the future, or that we should focus our efforts on learning flexibility so that women are well prepared for whatever the future throws at them. We consider the case for promoting planning first.

If we do not want to "blame the victim" and fall into the trap of believing in stereotypes of incompetence or irrationality among women, we can recall the voluminous literature recounting the limitations of normal human thinking. This literature specifically addresses the gap between what is most rational and what is actually done in problem solving and planning. The most common planning deficits found in psychological studies (conducted primarily by men on men) include failure to explore all possible alternatives, failure to consider all of the consequences of every alternative when deciding what to do, and failure to plan for contingencies.[5] Little surprise, then, to find some of these same problems among women planning their futures.

Because these failings are so common, and also occur in business and political arenas where errors may cost billions of dollars or thousands of lives, a great deal of thought has gone into devising ways to encourage rational decision making and planning. Some of these solutions could be adapted for use by women thinking about their career and family life planning. In most life planning instances, all possible alternatives and consequences are not known; hence, nonprogrammed planning processes would be more appropriate than the elaborate programmed decision systems used for some business decisions. In particular, group decision techniques such as brainstorming, nominal group or Delphi processes can be used to enable people to pool their knowledge and experience to develop plans that are less limited than any one person could do by herself.

In one sense, in PTA meetings and in professional networks, women often share their experiences in ways that could help them make better decisions. One thing an individual woman can do is to consciously seek out such interactions and raise the issue of the variety of life patterns among women. Professional or peer counselors can contribute to formal or informal gatherings by structuring opportunities for women with different experiences to participate in discussion sessions.

Women also can learn to use ways of interacting in a group to highlight and value differences. This maximizes the key role differences play in encouraging group members to consider a wider variety of alternatives. It also reduces the chances of falling into a trap of "group think," which limits the range of alternatives considered.

Another point of view, which emphasizes developing flexibility to prepare for a variety of contingencies in an ambiguous, rapidly changing world, might be a legitimate response to the evidence of the Breadwinners and Nesters, who changed their life plans in response to changes in themselves, their families, and their jobs. Responses to promote planning or to promote flexibility are not mutually exclusive. The same group discussions and valuing diversity techniques mentioned above as aiding detailed life planning also have the effect of broadening consideration of new alternatives and can lead to increased flexibility among those who do not develop specific future plans.

Contingency planning is another way of supporting flexibility that is included in sophisticated discussions of planning and that may be applied to choosing a life path. In this case, flexibility is promoted by developing scenarios for a range of alternatives and then working out when each scenario would be preferred, how options can be held open as long as possible, and what rules or criteria would be used to decide when to implement Plan B, or Plan C, instead of Plan A.

In the case of life pattern choices, every woman benefits when she considers each life pattern and works out the circumstances when each would be preferable, as well as the steps needed to maximize the benefits and minimize the drawbacks of each pattern. In addition, she could consider what circumstances would trigger a change in course and how to keep more than one option open as long as possible.

This way of thinking about paid work and home life is consistent both with trends in delaying marriage and childbearing and with career planning focused on a whole organization or a broad professional arena rather than on a specific job. It also fits contemporary organizational downsizing, which discourages commitment to a single organization.[6]

Gain Social Support

The last step that individuals who have clarified their preferences and planned for a flexible range of options need to consider is developing the social support of others who affirm their choices. Social support was tied to behavioral consistency whereas lack of support was tied to change, ambivalence, and dissatisfaction. True, we do not get to choose our parents, and parents do have a strong impact on children's preferences and perceived alternatives. But the evidence is strong that husbands, friends, co-workers, and bosses have an impact, and women have more adult choice in who these might be.

Some college students in the study were consciously thinking of what kind of husbands they wanted when they discussed their own plans for employment and family. However, most young men of the era did not share the egalitarian beliefs the young women desired. The future issue is the importance of considering similarity of beliefs about appropriate roles for men and women when making a decision about entering into a committed relationship. Creating group settings of young men and women of diverse viewpoints to discuss these issues is one way to encourage frank exchange between couples in a context where conflict can be moderated to reduce personalized attacks.

Seeking social support on the job for choices about combining employment and family appeared less often in statements made by women as college students, although some realized it was important and difficult to do. One lesson to learn from this study is that we need to encourage young women to consider explicitly how particular jobs or organizations are, or are not, likely to be supportive of their choices. Too often a blanket condemnation of "big business" as unfeeling and unsupportive of individual life choices serves as a reason to ignore or put less effort into such a search, when in fact variation does exist and could be matched to individual preferences. The role of employing organizations is discussed in more depth in the following section as we explore the range of alternatives available.

THE IMPLICATIONS FOR EMPLOYERS

The key issues for organizations when discussing women's employment-family life patterns are the same as those discussed for men—how to select, motivate, and retain employees who have the skills to meet the organization's goals effectively. Reports like Workforce 2000[7] emphasize that growth in the labor force will be greater among women than among men. Other reports emphasize the challenge of global competition for U.S. organizations and the need to develop strategic plans based on identifying a unique competitive advantage. We can use the results of this study to determine which organizational practices are effective, and which responses may need to vary from those commonly held in the past in order to achieve a competitive edge.

Screen and Select Legally

Sometimes secretly and sometimes openly, many managers have thought how much they would like to hire only men or only women with no family ties to distract them or make them leave their jobs.[8] Of course, in the real world this practice is both impossible and illegal; however, it is surprisingly persistent in discussions of selection of new employees, and disappointingly confirmed by studies of discrimination in careers of educated women.[9]

This study shows that selection is not an efficient way to solve work-family problems. As college students, the sample was almost evenly split between those who intended to leave the labor force after childbirth and those who planned to work more continuously. Although college intentions are the strongest predictor of later behavior, one would not want to use them as a selection criterion. The current sample is composed of one-third who intended to work continuously and did, one quarter who intended to quit and did, one-third who intended to quit and did not, and 7 percent who intended to work and quit. True, the respondents to the second phase of this study are not a precisely equal representation of the women as college students, but even taking into account the error due to differences in responding to a questionnaire a decade later, any organization that failed to hire women because the firm suspected they intended to quit when they had their first child would have lost a substantial number of potential "stayers."

Support Career Management

If selection is not the answer, then what can an organization do to work with those whom it has hired to encourage them to remain and work productively? Evidence from this study does not support the use of a "mommy track" in organizational career development. A "mommy track" presupposes that some employees do not wish a career characterized by upward mobility and commitment to the organization, but will choose early in their paid work life to forgo this alternative in order to have more time and energy to commit to their families.

This career alternative does not meet the needs of any one of the four groups in this study. The Careerists and the Breadwinners do not wish to give up traditional career mobility alternatives, even if their focus on job or family issues may wax or wane depending upon opportunities available in each sphere. The Nesters and Homemakers would be very likely to find that the kinds of jobs an organization might place in a "mommy track" excel in those characteristics that they found so unpleasant that they decided to stay at home. This response would defeat the purpose a "mommy track" was proposed to avoid: turnover of new mothers.

The other set of characteristics of "mommy track" jobs—increased flexibility of hours and options—were desired by *all* of the women in this study and are often desired by men as well. "Family friendly" corporate policies such as flexible work hours, job sharing, flexible leave policies for personal reasons, and consideration of personal needs in relocation options were universally requested by all members of the study, regardless of their individual plans for employment following childbirth. While maintenance of the label "family policy" may be politically expedient and these policies may be related to increasing productivity and reducing turnover, based on the finding of this study it would be fallacious to assume that the effects of family-friendly policies are solely or even primarily to reduce childbirth-related turnover. A more accurate term might be "humane policies"—policies that regard workers as full human beings with complex lives and increase productivity of all workers because their personal human realities are acknowledged. This recommendation is consistent with contemporary research on paid work and family integration, which suggests that competitive organizations may need "to evaluate and perhaps change the norms and values inherent in a given organizational culture about the 'appropriate' kind of interaction between work and personal life."[10]

In particular, corporate trainers and career managers could focus effort on finding ways to assist young employees to clarify their values and examine alternatives carefully. Mentor programs, career-focused discussion groups, and career management programs maximizing exposure to a large number of diverse people and a variety of available options address the need for more realistic information about the self and the world of paid work.[11]

Explicit career planning programs can meet the need for designing career plans with detailed action steps, consideration of alternatives, and contingency planning. The chief organizational consideration is whether or not organizations are prepared to offer career alternatives that match those desired by their employees. If they cannot, career planning programs may increase rather than decrease turnover if they reveal a mismatch between individual and organizational plans for a woman's future.[12]

Design Meaningful Jobs

Organizations can respond with policies that directly influence women to remain on the job following childbirth even if they had originally planned to leave. Providing challenging jobs with good salaries early in women's careers is most effective in this regard.

To be effective, exposure to a broad range of realistic options as part of a program of organizational career development must compare favorably to the alternative of child care and homemaking.[13] The bad news is that, in many cases, entry-level jobs may not meet this comparison favorably. The good news is that both homemaking and employment have a wide range of costs and benefits to be compared. Just as child care has the benefits of nurturing challenging development and creative child play as well as the costs of dirty diapers and baby talk, organizational jobs may be designed to include the benefits of challenge and creativity to counteract the burdens of responsibility or boredom.

Job enrichment is a common form of job design that concentrates on increasing challenge and responsibility of many jobs in an organization.

The role of job enrichment in increasing satisfaction and decreasing turnover is well established in a wide variety of studies,[14] but this book makes the connection to childbirth-related turnover. In research reported here, one of the most persuasive factors encouraging Breadwinners to stay with jobs after childbirth was work that was more challenging, creative, and financially rewarding than they expected. The challenge for organizations is to provide such work early in a young woman's career so that she can learn of this potential before she has her first child.

Encourage Social Support from Supervisors and Co-Workers

Social support among co-workers and supervisors influences women to remain at work after childbirth. Organizations adopting "family friendly" or "humane" policies may enable women and men to manage work and home roles in ways they desire; an indirect effect of these policies is signaling to women, as well as to men, that employment of parents is considered desirable in a particular organization.

The large impact of social support on this decision provides a strong argument for targeting all programs addressing family-work issues to men as well as women. Since many bosses and spouses are men and men, on average, are less supportive of employment of mothers, their views are a decisive contributor to childbirth-related turnover.[15] Even women who worked in "family friendly" organizations left *to find another job*, if their unsupportive supervisors disapproved of their personal choices. Furthermore, several recent studies have found that men are more likely than women to report negative spillover of family responsibilities into their work. In this case, *men* may need as much or more support for combining work and family roles. Both spouse and institutional support are needed for high life, work, and marital satisfaction among dual career couples.[16]

A growing number of women in upper levels of American companies have struggled in private with this issue because they perceived the subject as tabu. They might benefit also from permission to share their experiences and to learn of similarities and differences with their younger female and male colleagues.

Provide Child Care and Family Benefits Policies

Fortunately, the issue of most concern to mothers, child welfare, is also the one most overtly addressed by companies that support "family friendly" policies. An organization may play several roles in this regard. It may choose to be reactive, to move work-family conflict out of the office, or to be proactive, to ameliorate potential conflicts.[17]

The simplest role is to serve as information provider. Many people do not have accurate information about the effects of employment of mothers and fathers on their children and organizations might provide such information to its employees. Since most of this information focuses on the quality of child care and family interaction, a slightly more involved organization might also provide information about, or encourage participation in, day care programs with favorable environments for children, training in time management, or counseling programs that help families resolve paid work-family conflict. The most involved organizations might provide these services themselves. IBM, Apple, AT&T, Johnson and Johnson, and Merck are often cited as examples of organizations taking the lead in family issues. In the current competitive environment, managers are challenging every corporate expense and often target fringe benefit costs. Some organizations are responding by increasing involvement in these programs to reduce indirect turnover expenses and to increase worker productivity on the job; others are reducing these programs to reduce immediate expenses. Policies in this area are changing so rapidly that an organization intent on increasing profitability by both increasing productivity and reducing costs must compute a traditional cost-benefit analysis of whether it is most advantageous to provide these services themselves or promote use of existing services in the community. In either case, to remain competitive, the policy chosen must have as its ultimate criteria its effect on motivating every worker to contribute his or her best to meeting organizational goals and its effect on retaining the best workers. Organizations that ignore the role of children in men's and women's lives lose this competitive advantage. Organizations that do not provide time for employees to be parents also jeopardize their future workforce.[18]

Whether an organization provides information about availability or provides the service itself depends on individual industry and community circumstances, but most organizations benefit from carefully examining what is needed. Some forms of job enrichment, values clarification, career planning, mentoring, time management, and distribution of information about family services have been practiced in many organizations. Results of this study support more widespread use of such practices. Results also question decisions made in tough economic times to eliminate these practices or to so overload workers in a rush to increase productivity that the benefits of family friendly policies are overwhelmed by a flood of overwork.

Innovate to Reduce Turnover

This study also suggests new practices that may be explored by organizations truly intent on keeping valued employees. The majority of mothers in this study stated that they wanted to maintain contact with their job if they had found a rewarding one, and they wanted to stay in touch with their children, too. While this was primarily expressed in connection with a desire to have part-time work during the period immediately following childbirth and a desire to have increased opportunities to interact with their children through on site-day care later, these are not the only options. A few creative mothers and organizations have worked out individual arrangements that approach these goals, but the majority have not even begun to address these issues or have rejected them out of hand as expensive or inefficient.

In an era when nursery schools commonly have teaching computers used by two- and three-year-olds, when Local Area Networks (LANs) are widely used for interoffice communications, and when some workers rarely or never come to a central office, this point of view is badly outdated. The time has come to use these new technologies in creative ways to more efficiently link parents to their children and to their jobs.

Far-sighted organizations will focus their energies on proactively designing work arrangements that soften the borders between paid work and family and encourage mothers and fathers to design work roles that are synergistic with organizational and family responsibilities.[19] That is, team systems need to be developed that are flexible and depend on team members rather than single individuals. True team work and flexibility would encourage the highest levels of work involvement at the most challenging and crucial job demand times while children's needs are being well met by professional caretakers. At the same time, it would encourage the highest levels of family involvement when children are the most fun or have the most pressing needs for their parents.

Other work-restructuring alternatives may appear when firms challenge assumptions that make combining employment and family concerns difficult. Some firms have discovered that innovative work policies resulted in both more supportive "family friendly" policies *and* more productive work units.[20]

THE FUTURE: 30s AND 40s

Contrary to earlier views of adulthood as a steady state, formed when many died in their thirties or forties, we now recognize that development and change continue and extend throughout adulthood. We also recognize that social change has an impact on adult development to create unique life patterns for every cohort of individuals born in the same era. And, more recently, we have come to recognize that these developmental and historical changes may be different for men and women. If we look at common developmental patterns and recent historical trends, we may make a few guarded guesses about what lies ahead at home and at paid work for all of these women and for each of the different subgroups of women.

Self and Family Development

Theories of adult development suggest common life patterns that progress during adulthood from (1) periods of formation of a new view of the self-concept and set of relationships through (2) periods of integration of these ideas into a coherent whole, to (3) periods of transition when one's view of one's self and one's relationships is reevaluated and perhaps changed. As discussed in contemporary academic work, for example, in *Women's Career Development*[21] or in *The Handbook of Career Theory,*[22] these transitions and patterns typically differ for men and for women.

Biological clocks and social normative clocks suggest that the decade of "thirty-something" is the time for women in this study to have children and settle into an integration focused on the parental role. Developmental changes for mothers in this domain will focus on learning how to meet the differing developmental demands of children as all mature. The deeply focused attention on self-discovery begun during adolescence may not be resumed or may be shared with other concerns either until children become less dependent through their own growth or until social change provides a wider variety of means of caring for children's dependence beyond maternal care.

The social change models of development described in Chapter 1 indicate that women's adult development is influenced not only by biological and identity formation issues, but also by social change. These models suggest that women in each group will be affected by the social trends occurring as they mature.[23] Future issues likely to have an impact on these women include the increasing globalization and ethnic diversity of U.S. society, rapid changes in communication technology, and increasingly conservative political values. While the conservative political values reinforce the family-centered life styles of Nesters and Homemakers, exposure to increasing technology and diversity may occur more often in paid work settings inhabited by Careerists and Breadwinners.

If different aspects of social change are affecting groups differently, there may be increased risk of misunderstanding or conflict between those who make different life choices. Alternatively, if those now staying home with their children have less opportunity to keep up with social changes in technology use, it may be more difficult for them to return to the labor force when they want to. In spite of these difficulties, since they are surrounded by those with similar values and maybe reinforced by more conservative family values in the society, those who are home now may not face significant challenge to change their self-concept even though the society continues to change.

Employed Career Development

For previous cohorts of women who reduced their participation in the work force when children were young, the period of greatest occupational achievement occurred later in their lives when child care responsibilities were lower. For the current cohort, a greater diversity of developmental patterns may occur. During the first decade after college graduation, both men and women typically move a few times to find an organization that suits them, and organizational perceptions of fast-track stars are formulated. By the second decade, career paths are consolidated and realistic options become evident both to organizational planners and individuals. Because it is less common today to have one career in a single organization, we might expect such a process of evaluating fit and skills to reoccur in a repeating pattern in future decades. Within this cycle, however, consolidation of individual, specific job competencies and understanding of professions continue during their thirties even as the organizational venues change and individuals adjust their aspirations to the limited opportunities and many challenges of U.S. businesses today.

Different Future Challenges

The Homemakers and the Nesters have chosen to enter deeply into their family connections by withdrawing from the paid workforce after child-birth. Yet few of them indicate they will never again have employment. The key issues that challenge these women are how to define themselves as separate from their families and how to maintain previous career competencies or develop new ones while addressing their families' needs. This is more difficult because these women are violating a common contemporary norm that modern women should be able to "do it all." Also, only a few career retraining programs specifically address the needs of college graduates, so these women may need to be particularly resourceful in obtaining jobs when they are ready to reenter the workforce.

In some cases, especially among Nesters, health concerns of family members or of themselves keep women out of the work force and may prevent them from returning. These women may face particularly difficult financial support crises if their husbands' incomes cease to be adequate to meet their needs. Even if health issues are not involved, divorce or death may challenge some of these women to return to the labor force before they expect to do so.

The challenge for Breadwinners is somewhat different. These women feel connected to both work and family and expect satisfaction from both domains. The issue for these women is not how to maintain career skills or self-definition, but how to balance the growing time demands at work and at home. Most of these women are working, not out of a strong career ambition, but because they found paid work unexpectedly satisfying and rewarding. If the current overly demanding pressure for productivity in American firms continues, and their husbands keep their jobs, these women may opt out of the work force for a time in the future. If, on the other hand, even more exciting opportunities arise or their husbands lose their jobs, they may become more committed to a career than they ever imagined in their youth. The danger of continuing this balancing act is that Breadwinners may end up feeling that they never completely meet anyone's needs. The opportunity that balance provides is diversity and richness and the safety that if one domain is rocky for a time, some life satisfaction may be gained from the other roles.

The Careerists are struggling with slower career advancement than they expected and more value to family life than they expected. Because they have a long-term commitment to their careers, they are less likely than the Breadwinners to stay home for an extended period of time. They may choose to stay in the labor force but reduce their commitment to career advancement while their children are young. In the long term, the future challenge for these women is whether to start a new organization on their own or try their chances in a different existing organization. Unfortunately, because of continuing discrimination and baby-boom oversupply of managers at a time of organizational downsizing and flattening, mobility in *most* organizations may be restricted. Career growth may depend on expansion of responsibility or empowerment rather than rise in status.[24] All options have career risks, but any may seem preferable to career stagnation.

In addition to the distinctly different challenge facing each group of women, all participants share the complexities of living in a society where there is little consensus on how best to nurture children and how best to provide an adequate income for all its members.[25] Because of this lack of agreement, it will be difficult to forge a public policy initiative to support any single life pattern alternative or even a range of choices. As a consequence, most women will continue to negotiate individual solutions to the challenge of balancing employment and family roles, and many women will continue to find they need better health insurance, more pay, more training, and more job responsibility than they can negotiate on their own.

In the midst of ambiguity created by rapid social change and changing developmental tasks, most women have proved remarkably identity affirming in choosing social roles that met their needs and in finding approval from those close to them. While ambiguity and ambivalence remain as these women look into a changing future, most feel proud and satisfied with the lives they are creating.

NOTES

1. For example, see E. H. Burack, M. Albrecht, & H. Seitler. (1980). *A Woman's guide to career satisfaction*. Belmont, WA: Wadsworth; Landy, M. (1990). *Planning positive careers*. Englewood Cliffs, NJ: Prentice Hall.

2. J. V. Lerner & N. L. Galambos. (1991). *Employed mothers and their children*. New York: Garland. See especially the chapter "From maternal employment to child outcomes: Preexisting group differences and moderating variables" by M. J. Zaslow, B. A. Rabinovich, & J.T.D. Suwalsky, 237–282.

3. J. Kimmel. (1992). *Child care and the employment behavior of single and married mothers*. Kalamazoo, MI: W. E. Upjohn Institute, Staff Working Papers, 92–14.

4. J. A. Schneer & F. Reitman. (1993). Effects of alternate family structures on managerial career paths. *Academy of Management Journal, 36*, 830–843.

5. H. Simon. (1978). Rationality as a process and as product of thought. *American Economic Review, 68*, 1–16.

6. J. Brockner, S. Grover, & M. Blonder. (1988). Predictors of survivors' job involvement following layoffs: A field study. *Journal of Applied Psychology, 73*, 436–442.

7. *Outlook 2000*. (1990). Washington, DC: Bureau of Labor Statistics, Office of Employment Projections.

8. B. P. Noble. (1993, January 2). An increase in biases seen against pregnant workers: New mothers may be first targets in staff cuts. *New York Times*, 1, 39.

9. J. A. Schneer & F. Reitman. (1993). Effects of alternate family structures on managerial career paths. *Academy of Management Journal, 36*, 830–843; L. K. Stroh, J. M. Brett, & A. H. Reilly. (1992). All the right stuff: A comparison of female and male managers' career progression. *Journal of Applied Psychology, 77*, 251–260.

10. S. A. Lobel & E. R. Kossek (Eds.). (1995). *Managing diversity: Human resource strategies for transforming the workplace*. Cambridge, MA: Blackwell.

11. K. E. Kram & D. T. Hall. (in press). Mentoring in a context of diversity and turbulence. In S. Lobel & E. E. Kossek (Eds.), *Managing diversity: Human resource strategies for transforming the workplace*. London: Blackwell Publishers.

12. C. S. Granrose & J. D. Portwood. (1987). Matching individual career plans and organizational career management. *Academy of Management Journal, 30*, 699–720.

13. M. A. Griffin & J. E. Mathieu. (1993). *The role of comparisons in turnover related processes*. Paper presented at Academy of Management meeting, Atlanta.

14. J. G. Miller & K. G. Wheeler. (1992). Unraveling the mysteries of gender differences in intentions to leave the organization. *Journal of Organizational Behavior, 13*, 465–478.

15. T. J. Covin & C. C. Brush. (1991). An examination of male and female attitudes toward career and family issues. *Sex Roles, 25*, 393–415.

16. L. A. Gilbert. (1994). Current perspectives on dual-career families. *American Psychological Society, 3*, 101–105.

17. D. S. Carlson. (1995). *Proactive versus reactive approaches to work-family conflict: A human resource management perspective*. Unpublished manuscript.

18. N. Gardels. (Ed.). (1990). Prodigal parents: Family vs. the 80-hour work week. *New Perspectives Quarterly, 7*, whole issue.

19. D. S. Carlson. (1995). *Proactive versus reactive approaches to work-family conflict: A human resource management perspective*. Unpublished manuscript.

20. L. Bailyn. (1995, June). "Work-'family' partnership: A catalyst for change." Unpublished manuscript. Ford Foundation/Xerox Project.

21. B. A. Gutek & L. Larwood. (1986). *Women's career development*. Newbury Park, CA: Sage.

22. M. B. Arthur, D. T. Hall, & B. S. Lawrence. (1989). *Handbook of career theory*. Cambridge, Eng.: Cambridge University Press.

23. A. J. Stewart & J. M. Healy, Jr. (1989). Linking individual development and social changes. *American Psychologist, 44*, 30–42.

24. D. T. Hall & J. Richter (1992). Career gridlock: Baby boomers hit the wall. *Academy of Management Executive, 4*, 7–22.

25. N. Gardels. (Ed.). (1990). Prodigal parents: Family vs. the 80-hour work week. *New Perspectives Quarterly, 7*, whole issue.

Appendix

PHASE I QUESTIONNAIRE: EMPLOYMENT AFTER CHILDBIRTH

Recently, many women have been combining paid employment and motherhood. There are different opinions about whether or not this is a good thing to do. On the following pages I would like to give you the opportunity to tell me what you think would happen if you worked or did not work during the first three years after the birth of your first child.

Whenever the term "work" is used in this questionnaire it means paid employment of ten or more hours per week done outside the home.

It is important that you answer *every* question. If you are not sure how you feel about something on one of the rating scales, circle your best guess. You may indicate that you are not sure by putting a "?" beside your answer. If you do not have enough room on a page to complete an answer, or if you would like to comment more fully on a particular question, you may use the space on the back cover.

Many questions ask you to rate—on a 5-point scale—how likely it is for something to occur. The numbers are:

1—almost no chance of occurring

2—about a 25% chance of occurring

3—about an equal chance of occurring, or not occurring

4—about a 75% chance of occurring

5—almost certain to occur

1) How likely is it that you will work during the first three years after childbirth?

VERY UNLIKELY
1
2
3
4
5
VERY LIKELY

2) How likely is it that you will NOT WORK during the first three years after childbirth?

VERY UNLIKELY
1
2
3
4
5
VERY LIKELY

On the following page is a list of things that might influence your decision to work following childbirth. You will be asked to rate the items on this list in three different ways. First, how much you value them and then how likely they are to occur. Please work carefully but quickly. You should be able to complete the page in a few minutes. If you are not married, please rate questions about your husband as if you were married.

3) This is a list of things that may influence your intentions to work following childbirth. Please consider how much you would like each item to be a part of your life. If you would never want this to be a part of your life you should circle a 1. (Please circle one number only for each item.)

RANK		EXTREMELY UNDESIRABLE				EXTREMELY DESIRABLE
_____ HAVING FUN		1	2	3	4	5
_____ A SENSE OF ACCOMPLISHMENT		1	2	3	4	5
_____ FEELING TIED DOWN		1	2	3	4	5
_____ HAVING VARIETY IN MY LIFE		1	2	3	4	5
_____ FEELING GUILTY		1	2	3	4	5
_____ FEELING RESENTFUL		1	2	3	4	5
_____ FEELING TIRED		1	2	3	4	5
_____ FEELING BORED		1	2	3	4	5
_____ FEELING CLOSE TO MY HUSBAND		1	2	3	4	5

_____ FEELING CLOSE TO MY CHILD	1	2	3	4	5
_____ RUNNING MY HOUSEHOLD SMOOTHLY	1	2	3	4	5
_____ TRAINING MY CHILD MYSELF	1	2	3	4	5
_____ MAINTAINING MY CAREER SKILLS	1	2	3	4	5
_____ MAINTAINING MY JOB CONTACTS	1	2	3	4	5
_____ ADVANCING MY CAREER	1	2	3	4	5
_____ EARNING ENOUGH INCOME MYSELF	1	2	3	4	5
_____ HAVING ENOUGH FAMILY INCOME	1	2	3	4	5
_____ HAVING EXTRA INCOME	1	2	3	4	5
_____ MAKING MORE $ THAN IT COSTS ME TO WORK	1	2	3	4	5
_____ HUSBAND NEEDING TWO JOBS	1	2	3	4	5
_____ MISSING CHILD'S GROWTH MILESTONES	1	2	3	4	5
_____ FINDING ADEQUATE CHILD CARE	1	2	3	4	5
_____ HAVING ENOUGH TIME FOR THE CHILD	1	2	3	4	5
_____ HAVING ENOUGH TIME FOR MYSELF	1	2	3	4	5
_____ HAVING ENOUGH TIME FOR MY HUSBAND	1	2	3	4	5
_____ HUSBAND HELPING AROUND THE HOUSE	1	2	3	4	5
_____ CHILD WILL BE INDEPENDENT	1	2	3	4	5
_____ CHILD WILL BE SECURE	1	2	3	4	5
_____ CHILD WILL BE WELL DISCIPLINED	1	2	3	4	5
_____ CHILD WILL GET ALONG EASILY WITH OTHERS	1	2	3	4	5
_____ CHILD WILL LEARN MY BELIEFS	1	2	3	4	5
_____ CHILD WILL FEEL LOVED	1	2	3	4	5
_____ CHILD WILL HAVE ATTENTION WHEN NEEDED	1	2	3	4	5
_____ CHILD FEELS CLOSER TO OTHERS THAN TO ME	1	2	3	4	5

Now please go back over this list and rank from 1 to 5 the five consequences that would most influence you in deciding whether or not to work after childbirth. Place a 1 in front of the most influential consequence, a 2 in front of the next, etc. You should rank only five consequences.

4) Are there any consequences, other than the ones on the preceding page, that might influence your decision to work or not to work during the first three years after childbirth? If so, please list them.

5) Please list any conditions that would make you DEFINITELY decide TO WORK during the first three years after childbirth, no matter what other consequences might exist.

How likely is it that these things might occur?

VERY UNLIKELY
1
2
3
4
5
VERY LIKELY

6) Now, list any conditions that would make you DEFINITELY decide NOT TO WORK during the first three years after childbirth, no matter what other consequences might exist.

How likely is it that these things might occur?

VERY UNLIKELY
1
2
3
4
5
VERY LIKELY

7) Do you have any "rules of thumb" that you would use to decide whether or not to work during the first three years after childbirth? If so, what are they?

8) Please list any consequences that are *more* likely to occur if you work PART TIME rather than FULL TIME during the first three years after childbirth.

9) Finally, list any consequences that are *less* likely to occur if you work PART TIME rather than FULL TIME during the first three years after childbirth.

CONSEQUENCES OF WORKING

10) Please rate the likelihood that each of the items on this list will occur if you WORK DURING THE FIRST THREE YEARS after the birth of your child. (Circle just one number per item.)

	VERY UNLIKELY				VERY LIKELY
_____ HAVING FUN	1	2	3	4	5
_____ A SENSE OF ACCOMPLISHMENT	1	2	3	4	5
_____ FEELING TIED DOWN	1	2	3	4	5
_____ HAVING VARIETY IN MY LIFE	1	2	3	4	5
_____ FEELING GUILTY	1	2	3	4	5

_____ FEELING RESENTFUL	1	2	3	4	5
_____ FEELING TIRED	1	2	3	4	5
_____ FEELING BORED	1	2	3	4	5
_____ FEELING CLOSE TO MY HUSBAND	1	2	3	4	5
_____ FEELING CLOSE TO MY CHILD	1	2	3	4	5
_____ RUNNING MY HOUSEHOLD SMOOTHLY	1	2	3	4	5
_____ TRAINING MY CHILD MYSELF	1	2	3	4	5
_____ MAINTAINING MY CAREER SKILLS	1	2	3	4	5
_____ MAINTAINING MY JOB CONTACTS	1	2	3	4	5
_____ ADVANCING MY CAREER	1	2	3	4	5
_____ EARNING ENOUGH INCOME MYSELF	1	2	3	4	5
_____ HAVING ENOUGH FAMILY INCOME	1	2	3	4	5
_____ HAVING EXTRA INCOME	1	2	3	4	5
_____ MAKING MORE $ THAN IT COSTS ME TO WORK	1	2	3	4	5
_____ HUSBAND NEEDING TWO JOBS	1	2	3	4	5
_____ MISSING CHILD'S GROWTH MILESTONES	1	2	3	4	5
_____ FINDING ADEQUATE CHILD CARE	1	2	3	4	5
_____ HAVING ENOUGH TIME FOR THE CHILD	1	2	3	4	5
_____ HAVING ENOUGH TIME FOR MYSELF	1	2	3	4	5
_____ HAVING ENOUGH TIME FOR MY HUSBAND	1	2	3	4	5
_____ HUSBAND HELPING AROUND THE HOUSE	1	2	3	4	5
_____ CHILD WILL BE INDEPENDENT	1	2	3	4	5
_____ CHILD WILL BE SECURE	1	2	3	4	5
_____ CHILD WILL BE WELL DISCIPLINED	1	2	3	4	5
_____ CHILD WILL GET ALONG EASILY WITH OTHERS	1	2	3	4	5
_____ CHILD WILL LEARN MY BELIEFS	1	2	3	4	5
_____ CHILD WILL FEEL LOVED	1	2	3	4	5
_____ CHILD WILL HAVE ATTENTION WHEN NEEDED	1	2	3	4	5
_____ CHILD FEELS CLOSER TO OTHERS THAN TO ME	1	2	3	4	5

CONFLICTING PLANS

I would now like you to consider whether plans that you may have in one area of your life might change the plans that you might have in another area of your life. (Circle ALL that apply.)

11) Because of my career goals, I plan to:

1. HAVE FEWER CHILDREN THAN I MIGHT OTHERWISE PREFER.

2. HAVE MORE CHILDREN THAN I MIGHT OTHERWISE PREFER.

3. HAVE MY FIRST CHILD LATER THAN I MIGHT OTHERWISE PREFER.

4. HAVE MY CHILDREN FURTHER APART THAN I MIGHT OTHERWISE PREFER.

5. HAVE MY CHILDREN CLOSER TOGETHER THAN I MIGHT OTHERWISE PREFER.

6. MY CAREER PLANS DO NOT INFLUENCE MY CHILDBEARING PLANS.

12) Because of the number of children I want, I plan to:

1. DO LESS FULL-TIME WORK THAN I MIGHT OTHERWISE PREFER.

2. DO MORE PART-TIME WORK THAN I MIGHT OTHERWISE PREFER.

3. DO LESS PART-TIME WORK THAN I MIGHT OTHERWISE PREFER.

4. CHOOSE A DIFFERENT KIND OF OCCUPATION THAN I MIGHT OTHERWISE PREFER.

5. CHOOSE A DIFFERENT JOB SITUATION THAN I MIGHT OTHERWISE PREFER.

6. MY CHILDBEARING PLANS DO NOT INFLUENCE MY CAREER PLANS.

13) Because of my intention to have my first child at a certain time, I have planned to:

1. DO MORE FULL-TIME WORK THAN I MIGHT OTHERWISE PREFER.

2. DO LESS FULL-TIME WORK THAN I MIGHT OTHERWISE PREFER.

3. DO MORE PART-TIME WORK THAN I MIGHT OTHERWISE PREFER.

4. CHOOSE A DIFFERENT JOB SITUATION THAN I MIGHT OTHERWISE PREFER.

5. MY CHILDBEARING PLANS DO NOT INFLUENCE MY CAREER PLANS.

14) Because of my intention to have my children a certain number of years apart, I have planned to:

1. DO MORE FULL-TIME WORK THAN I MIGHT OTHERWISE PREFER.

2. DO LESS FULL-TIME WORK THAN I MIGHT OTHERWISE PREFER.

3. DO MORE PART-TIME WORK THAN I MIGHT OTHERWISE PREFER.

4. DO LESS PART-TIME WORK THAN I MIGHT OTHERWISE PREFER.

5. CHOOSE A DIFFERENT JOB SITUATION THAN I MIGHT OTHERWISE PREFER.

6. MY CHILDBEARING PLANS DO NOT INFLUENCE MY CAREER PLANS.

CONSEQUENCES OF NOT WORKING

This is the last time you will be asked to rate the items on this list.

15) How likely is it that each of these things will occur if you DO NOT WORK AT ALL DURING THE FIRST THREE YEARS after the birth of your child? (Circle one number for each item.)

	VERY UNLIKELY				VERY LIKELY
HAVING FUN	1	2	3	4	5
A SENSE OF ACCOMPLISHMENT	1	2	3	4	5
FEELING TIED DOWN	1	2	3	4	5
HAVING VARIETY IN MY LIFE	1	2	3	4	5
FEELING GUILTY	1	2	3	4	5
FEELING RESENTFUL	1	2	3	4	5
FEELING TIRED	1	2	33	4	5
FEELING BORED	1	2	3	4	5
FEELING CLOSE TO MY HUSBAND	1	2	3	4	5
FEELING CLOSE TO MY CHILD	1	2	3	4	5
RUNNING MY HOUSEHOLD SMOOTHLY	1	2	3	4	5
TRAINING MY CHILD MYSELF	1	2	3	4	5
MAINTAINING MY CAREER SKILLS	1	2	3	4	5
MAINTAINING MY JOB CONTACTS	1	2	3	4	5
ADVANCING MY CAREER	1	2	3	4	5
EARNING ENOUGH INCOME MYSELF	1	2	3	4	5
HAVING ENOUGH FAMILY INCOME	1	2	3	4	5
HAVING EXTRA INCOME	1	2	3	4	5
MAKING MORE $ THAN IT COSTS ME TO WORK	1	2	3	4	5
HUSBAND NEEDING TWO JOBS	1	2	3	4	5
MISSING CHILD'S GROWTH MILESTONES	1	2	3	4	5
FINDING ADEQUATE CHILD CARE	1	2	3	4	5
HAVING ENOUGH TIME FOR THE CHILD	1	2	3	4	5
HAVING ENOUGH TIME FOR MYSELF	1	2	3	4	5
HAVING ENOUGH TIME FOR MY HUSBAND	1	2	3	4	5
HUSBAND HELPING AROUND THE HOUSE	1	2	3	4	5

CHILD WILL BE INDEPENDENT	1	2	3	4	5
CHILD WILL BE SECURE	1	2	3	4	5
CHILD WILL BE WELL DISCIPLINED	1	2	3	4	5
CHILD WILL GET ALONG EASILY WITH OTHERS	1	2	3	4	5
CHILD WILL LEARN MY BELIEFS	1	2	3	4	5
CHILD WILL FEEL LOVED	1	2	3	4	5
CHILD WILL HAVE ATTENTION WHEN NEEDED	1	2	3	4	5
CHILD FEELS CLOSER TO OTHERS THAN TO ME	1	2	3	4	5

PLANS

All of the previous questions have assumed that you have a fairly definite idea about what you want in the future. In fact, while many people prefer to have a very specific plan for the future, others prefer to live as spontaneously as possible. Please describe the extent of your plans related to work and family.

16) Do you have a specific goal for your career? (Circle one number.)

1. I DO NOT HAVE ANY PARTICULAR GOAL AND I DO NOT WANT ONE.
2. I HAVE A GENERAL IDEA BUT NO SPECIFIC GOAL.
3. I HAVE A SPECIFIC GOAL.

17) If you have a specific goal, what is it?
18) Do you have a strategy for achieving this goal? (Circle one.)

1. I HAVE NO PARTICULAR STRATEGY AND I DO NOT WANT ONE.
2. I HAVE A GENERAL IDEA BUT NO SPECIFIC STRATEGY.
3. I HAVE A SPECIFIC STRATEGY.

19) What are the main features of your strategy, if you have one?

Do you foresee anything that might prevent you from carrying out your plan?

If your plans are blocked, do you have any alternative plans? If so, please list them.

20) How far into the future does your career plan extend? (Circle one.)

1. I PREFER TO LIVE MY LIFE ONE DAY AT A TIME.
2. THE NEXT YEAR.
3. THE NEXT TWO TO FIVE YEARS.
4. THE NEXT SIX TO TEN YEARS.
5. MORE THAN TEN YEARS.

21) Do you have any specific goal for how you want to raise your children? (Circle one.)

1. I DO NOT HAVE ANY PARTICULAR GOAL AND I DO NOT WANT ONE.

2. I HAVE A GENERAL IDEA BUT NO SPECIFIC GOAL.

3. I HAVE A SPECIFIC GOAL.

22) If you have such a goal, what is it?

23) Do you have a strategy for achieving your childrearing goals?

1. I HAVE NO PARTICULAR STRATEGY AND I DO NOT WANT ONE.

2. I HAVE A GENERAL IDEA BUT NO SPECIFIC STRATEGY.

3. I HAVE A SPECIFIC STRATEGY.

24) What are the main features of your childrearing strategy, if you have one?
   Do you foresee anything that might prevent you from implementing your plan?
   If your plans are blocked, do you have any alternative plans?

25) How far into the future does your childrearing plan extend?

1. I PREFER TO LIVE MY LIFE ONE DAY AT A TIME.

2. THE NEXT YEAR.

3. THE NEXT TWO TO FIVE YEARS.

4. THE NEXT SIX TO TEN YEARS.

5. MORE THAN TEN YEARS.

26) Do you have a specific plan for combining work and childrearing?

1. I DO NOT HAVE ANY PARTICULAR GOAL AND I DO NOT WANT ONE.

2. I HAVE A GENERAL IDEA BUT NO SPECIFIC GOAL.

3. I HAVE A SPECIFIC GOAL.

27) What are the main features of your plan, if you have one?
   Do you foresee anything that might prevent you from implementing your plan?
   If your plans are blocked, do you have any alternative plans?

INFLUENCE OF OTHERS

28) For many people, the opinions of their parents, friends or husband may be important in making decisions. Indicate how likely these people are to approve of your working during the first three years after childbirth. Also indicate how likely you are to do as they wish. If there are other people whose opinions are important to you in making this decision, please write in their relationship to you (not their name) and indicate their opinion and your reaction in the extra spaces provided below.

PERSON (relationship)	OPINION					PROBABILITY				
	VERY LIKELY TO DISAPPROVE			VERY LIKELY TO APPROVE		I AM UNLIKELY TO DO AS THEY WISH			I AM LIKELY TO DO AS THEY WISH	
1. mother	1	2	3	4	5	1	2	3	4	5
2. father	1	2	3	4	5	1	2	3	4	5
3. husband	1	2	3	4	5	1	2	3	4	5
4. best friend	1	2	3	4	5	1	2	3	4	5
5. _____	1	2	3	4	5	1	2	3	4	5
6. _____	1	2	3	4	5	1	2	3	4	5

29) In what way has the observation of your mother's life influenced your own plans about working and having children?

30) Was your mother satisfied with her choice of working or not working? (Circle one)

      VERY UNSATISFIED
          1
          2
          3
          4
          5
      VERY SATISFIED

31) Was your father satisfied with your mother's choice? (Circle one)

      VERY UNSATISFIED
          1
          2
          3
          4
          5
      VERY SATISFIED

32) If there have been other people who have been important to you in deciding your plans for work and childbearing, please identify them. (For example, sister, aunt, neighbor, teacher, grandmother.)

33) What did you learn from them?

34) Getting ahead in life is mostly a matter of luck.

    1. AGREE STRONGLY
    2. AGREE SLIGHTLY

3. DISAGREE SLIGHTLY
4. DISAGREE STRONGLY
5. DON'T KNOW

35) It is not always wise to plan too far ahead because many things turn out to be a matter of good or bad fortune anyway.

1. AGREE STRONGLY
2. AGREE SLIGHTLY
3. DISAGREE SLIGHTLY
4. DISAGREE STRONGLY
5. DON'T KNOW

36) Many times I feel that I have little influence over the things that happen to me.

1. AGREE STRONGLY
2. AGREE SLIGHTLY
3. DISAGREE SLIGHTLY
4. DISAGREE STRONGLY
5. DON'T KNOW

37) When I make plans, I am almost certain I can make them work.

1. AGREE STRONGLY
2. AGREE SLIGHTLY
3. DISAGREE SLIGHTLY
4. DISAGREE STRONGLY
5. DON'T KNOW

PREVIOUS EXPERIENCE

38) How often did you baby sit for families other than your own when you were growing up? (Circle one)

1. NEVER
2. A FEW TIMES
3. MONTHLY
4. WEEKLY
5. MORE THAN ONCE A WEEK

39) How much time did you spend caring for brothers and sisters when you were growing up? (Circle one)

1. NEVER
2. OCCASIONALLY

    3. ONCE OR TWICE A WEEK

    4. ALMOST EVERY DAY

    5. SEVERAL HOURS EACH DAY

40) How often did you have a chance to talk with a person who is doing the job you hope to do?

    1. I HAVE NOT YET DECIDED WHAT KIND OF WORK I WANT TO DO

    2. NEVER

    3. ONCE OR TWICE

    4. SEVERAL TIMES

    5. OFTEN

41) How often did you have a chance to observe a person working at what you want to do?

    1. I HAVE NOT YET DECIDED WHAT KIND OF WORK I WANT TO DO

    2. NEVER

    3. ONCE OR TWICE

    4. SEVERAL TIMES

    5. OFTEN

42) Please describe each job you have held for more than two consecutive weeks since you were fourteen years old.

	KIND OF WORK	AGE BEGUN	NUMBER OF MONTHS	HOURS PER WEEK
FIRST JOB				
NEXT JOB				
NEXT JOB				
NEXT JOB				
NEXT JOB				
NEXT JOB				
CURRENT JOB				

43) Even though you may not have a clear idea of what you want to do in the future, please describe the kinds of jobs you think you will have in the future. Begin with the next job you expect to have. If there are some periods when you intend to not work, record "No Work" in the first column and fill out the duration of "No Work" in the next 2 columns. If you intend to work only part of the year, please use fractions, i.e., 1/12, etc.

WHAT KIND OF WORK WILL YOU DO?	HOW OLD WILL YOU BE WHEN YOU START THIS JOB?	HOW MANY YEARS WILL YOU WORK?	HOW MANY HRS/WK DO YOU INTEND TO WORK?
NEXT JOB			
NEXT JOB			
NEXT JOB			
NEXT JOB			
NEXT JOB			

BACKGROUND

44) Was your mother born in the United States? (Circle one)
1. YES
2. NO _____
   Country of Birth

45) Was your father born in the United States?
1. YES
2. NO _____
   Country of Birth

46) What was the highest grade of regular school your father completed?

47) What was the highest grade of regular school your mother completed?

48) For every period that you lived in the same household with your father and/or your mother, please record the main kind of work they did and the number of hours/week they worked outside the home. If they were not working, write in "NO WORK." If they worked at home write in "AT HOME" and the kind of job and the hours. If you were not living with them write in "ABSENT."

YOUR AGE	MOTHER		FATHER	
	MOTHER'S OCCUPATION	#HRS. MOTHER WORKED/WEEK	FATHER'S OCCUPATION	#HRS. FATHER WORKED/WEEK
Birth–3				
3–5				
6–12				
13–Present				

49) How old are you?

50) How old is each of your brothers?

51) How old is each of your sisters?

52) What is your religious preference? (Circle one)

    1. PROTESTANT
    2. CATHOLIC
    3. JEWISH
    4. OTHER
    5. NONE

53) Where did you live most of the time before college? (Circle one)
    1. ON A FARM
    2. IN THE COUNTRY, BUT NOT ON A FARM
    3. IN A TOWN OR SMALL CITY
    4. IN A LARGE CITY (population over 100,000)

54) What is the highest grade of regular school (including college) you have ever attended?

55) As it stands now, how much more education do you think you will actually get? (Circle one)
    1. LESS THAN FOUR YEARS OF COLLEGE
    2. GRADUATE FROM A FOUR-YEAR COLLEGE
    3. OBTAIN A MASTER'S DEGREE
    4. OBTAIN A PROFESSIONAL DEGREE (M.D., LAW, ETC.)
    5. OBTAIN A PH.D.

56) What is your current marital status? How long has this been your status?
    1. NO LONG-TERM RELATIONSHIP WITH A MAN   _____
    2. LIVING PARTNER   _____
    3. ENGAGED   _____
    4. MARRIED   _____
    5. DIVORCED   _____
    6. OTHER   _____

57) If you have a long-term relationship with a man, what is his occupation? If he is currently a student, what is his intended occupation?

58) Realistically speaking, how many children do you think you will have when your family is complete?

_____ BORN TO ME   PLUS _____ ADOPTED

59) If you already have children, how old is each of your daughters?

60) If you already have children, how old is each of your sons?

61) How soon do you intend to (or did you) return to work after the birth of your first child?

62) If you do not have children, how old will you be when you have (or adopt) your first child?

63) How many years apart have you had, or do you intend to have, your children?
_____ NUMBER OF YEARS BETWEEN THE FIRST AND SECOND
_____ NUMBER OF YEARS BETWEEN THE SECOND AND THIRD
_____ NUMBER OF YEARS BETWEEN THE THIRD AND FOURTH

64) What do you expect to be (or what was) your husband's annual income at the time of the birth of your first child? $ _____

65) What do you expect to be (or was) your own annual income at the time of the birth of your first child? $ _____

  * If you have any further comments, you may use the back cover of the questionnaire.

  * Thank you for your time and patience in contributing to this research effort.

  * Place the questionnaire in the envelope provided.

  * SEAL THE ENVELOPE.

  * Place the envelope in the U.S. Mail.

PHASE II QUESTIONNAIRE: EMPLOYMENT FOLLOWING CHILDBIRTH

Recently, many women have been combining paid employment and motherhood. There are different opinions about whether or not this is a good thing to do. We are interested in your *personal* opinion. Circle the answer that reflects your own beliefs.

There are some questions for those who are working and others for those who are not. Whenever the term "work" is used in this questionnaire it means paid employment of ten hours per week or more. Please follow directions to answer or to skip questions carefully.

Some questions ask you to talk about the time immediately before or after the birth of your first child. If you have not yet had a child answer about your current situation. Many questions ask you to rate—on a 5-point scale—how likely it is for something to occur. The numbers are:

1—almost no chance of occurring

2—about a 25% chance of occurring

3—about an equal chance of occurring, or not occurring

4—about a 75% chance of occurring

5—almost certain to occur

1. If you have already had or adopted a child, when did this first occur?

(1) _____ (2) I DO NOT HAVE A CHILD (IF NOT GO TO Q #4)
DAY/MO/YR

2. If you have already had or adopted a child, have you had paid employment since that time? (1) NO (2) YES
If yes, when did you return to work after this birth or adoption?
_____DAY/MO/YR

3. If you have more than one child, what is the date of birth of each of your children after the first one? (ANSWER, THEN PLEASE GO TO Q #6)
_____DAY/MO/YR_____DAY/MO/YR_____DAY/MO/YR_____DAY/MO/YR

4. If you have not yet had a child, do you ever intend to have one?
(1) YES   (2) NO   (IF NO, RETURN THIS QUESTIONNAIRE NOW)
If yes, about how many years from now would you like to become a mother?
_____YEARS FROM NOW

5. How likely is it that you will work during the first three years after childbirth?
1   2   3   4   5
VERY UNLIKELY   VERY LIKELY

6. How likely is it that you will *not* work during the first three years after childbirth?
1   2   3   4   5
VERY UNLIKELY   VERY LIKELY

VALUES

7. Please consider how much you would like each of the following items to be a part of your life. If something is valuable to you, you might circle a 4, or even a 5. If, on the other hand, you would never want this to be a part of your life, you should circle a 1. (Please circle one number only for each item.)

CONSEQUENCES	EXTREMELY UNDESIRABLE				EXTREMELY DESIRABLE
HAVING FUN	1	2	3	4	5
A SENSE OF ACCOMPLISHMENT	1	2	3	4	5
FEELING TIED DOWN	1	2	3	4	5
HAVING VARIETY IN MY LIFE	1	2	3	4	5
FEELING GUILTY	1	2	3	4	5
FEELING RESENTFUL	1	2	3	4	5
FEELING TIRED	1	2	3	4	5
FEELING BORED	1	2	3	4	5
FEELING CLOSE TO MY HUSBAND	1	2	3	4	5
FEELING CLOSE TO MY CHILD	1	2	3	4	5

RUNNING MY HOUSEHOLD SMOOTHLY	1	2	3	4	5
TRAINING MY CHILD MYSELF	1	2	3	4	5
MAINTAINING MY CAREER SKILLS	1	2	3	4	5
MAINTAINING MY JOB CONTACTS	1	2	3	4	5
ADVANCING MY CAREER	1	2	3	4	5
EARNING ENOUGH INCOME MYSELF	1	2	3	4	5
HAVING ENOUGH FAMILY INCOME	1	2	3	4	5
HAVING EXTRA INCOME	1	2	3	4	5
MAKING MORE $ THAN IT COSTS ME TO WORK	1	2	3	4	5
HUSBAND NEEDING TWO JOBS	1	2	3	4	5
MISSING CHILD'S GROWTH MILESTONES	1	2	3	4	5
FINDING ADEQUATE CHILD CARE	1	2	3	4	5
HAVING ENOUGH TIME FOR THE CHILD	1	2	3	4	5
HAVING ENOUGH TIME FOR MYSELF	1	2	3	4	5
HAVING ENOUGH TIME FOR MY HUSBAND	1	2	3	4	5
HUSBAND HELPING AROUND THE HOUSE	1	2	3	4	5
CHILD WILL BE INDEPENDENT	1	2	3	4	5
CHILD WILL BE SECURE	1	2	3	4	5
CHILD WILL BE WELL DISCIPLINED	1	2	3	4	5
CHILD WILL GET ALONG EASILY WITH OTHERS	1	2	3	4	5
CHILD WILL DO BETTER IN SCHOOL	1	2	3	4	5
CHILD WILL FEEL LOVED	1	2	3	4	5
CHILD WILL HAVE ATTENTION WHEN NEEDED	1	2	3	4	5
CHILD FEELS CLOSER TO OTHERS THAN TO ME	1	2	3	4	5
CHILD WILL BELIEVE WOMEN ARE COMPETENT	1	2	3	4	5

8. Now go back and rank order into the *five most* important in your decision to work following childbirth, 1=most important. Rank *only* five consequences.

Thinking about the time you were (will be) considering becoming a mother, in making your decision about combining your career and childbearing, please answer the following questions. If you need more room, use the inside cover of the questionnaire.

9. What factors did (or will) you consider and how did (will) each factor influence you to stay home or return to work quickly after the birth of your first child?

10. What process did (will) you use to make this decision? (Whom will you talk to, how will you decide?)

11. Realistically, how old do you think a child should be for his or her mother to start working full time?   Why this age?

12. Is there anything your employing organization could do (have done) that will (would) make you more likely to return to work following childbirth? If so, what?
    What would make you more likely to leave and not come back?

CONSEQUENCES OF WORKING

13. Please rate the likelihood that each of the items on this list might occur if you WORKED DURING THE FIRST THREE YEARS after the birth of your first child. (Circle one number per item. If you have no child or did not work, answer hypothetically.)

	VERY UNLIKELY			VERY LIKELY
HAVING FUN	1	2	3	4	5
A SENSE OF ACCOMPLISHMENT	1	2	3	4	5
FEELING TIED DOWN	1	2	3	4	5
HAVING VARIETY IN MY LIFE	1	2	3	4	5
FEELING GUILTY	1	2	3	4	5
FEELING RESENTFUL	1	2	3	4	5
FEELING TIRED	1	2	3	4	5
FEELING BORED	1	2	3	4	5
FEELING CLOSE TO MY HUSBAND	1	2	3	4	5
FEELING CLOSE TO MY CHILD	1	2	3	4	5
RUNNING MY HOUSEHOLD SMOOTHLY	1	2	3	4	5
TRAINING MY CHILD MYSELF	1	2	3	4	5
MAINTAINING MY CAREER SKILLS	1	2	3	4	5
MAINTAINING MY JOB CONTACTS	1	2	3	4	5
ADVANCING MY CAREER	1	2	3	4	5
EARNING ENOUGH INCOME MYSELF	1	2	3	4	5
HAVING ENOUGH FAMILY INCOME	1	2	3	4	5

HAVING EXTRA INCOME	1	2	3	4	5
MAKING MORE $ THAN IT COSTS ME TO WORK	1	2	3	4	5
HUSBAND NEEDING TWO JOBS	1	2	3	4	5
MISSING CHILD'S GROWTH MILESTONES	1	2	3	4	5
FINDING ADEQUATE CHILD CARE	1	2	3	4	5
HAVING ENOUGH TIME FOR THE CHILD	1	2	3	4	5
HAVING ENOUGH TIME FOR MYSELF	1	2	3	4	5
HAVING ENOUGH TIME FOR MY HUSBAND	1	2	3	4	5
HUSBAND HELPING AROUND THE HOUSE	1	2	3	4	5
CHILD WILL BE INDEPENDENT	1	2	3	4	5
CHILD WILL BE SECURE	1	2	3	4	5
CHILD WILL BE WELL DISCIPLINED	1	2	3	4	5
CHILD WILL GET ALONG EASILY WITH OTHERS	1	2	3	4	5
CHILD WILL DO BETTER IN SCHOOL	1	2	3	4	5
CHILD WILL FEEL LOVED	1	2	3	4	5
CHILD WILL HAVE ATTENTION WHEN NEEDED	1	2	3	4	5
CHILD FEELS CLOSER TO OTHERS THAN TO ME	1	2	3	4	5
CHILD WILL BELIEVE WOMEN ARE COMPETENT	1	2	3	4	5

FEELINGS ABOUT YOURSELF

14. For the following questions, circle the numer that corresponds to how much you agree or disagree.

Strongly Disagree	Disagree	Neither Agree nor Disagree	Agree	Strongly Agree
1	2	3	4	5

a.	I feel that I'm a person of worth at least on an equal basis with others.	1	2	3	4	5
b.	I am able to do things as well as most other people.	1	2	3	4	5
c.	I certainly feel useless at times.	1	2	3	4	5

d. Problems are easy to solve once you understand   1   2   3   4   5
    the various consequences of your actions.

e. I would make a fine model for an apprentice   1   2   3   4   5
    to learn the skills she/he would need to
    succeed.

f. If anyone can find the answer, I'm the one.   1   2   3   4   5

g. My talents, or where I can concentrate my   1   2   3   4   5
    attention best, are found in areas not related to
    this job.

h. Mastering my job doesn't mean much to me.   1   2   3   4   5

i. It is important to me to be seen by others as   1   2   3   4   5
    very successful.

j. I very badly want to "make my mark" in my   1   2   3   4   5
    career.

k. I am very satisfied with my career.   1   2   3   4   5

l. I am very satisfied with the intimate   1   2   3   4   5
    relationships in my life.

m. I am very satisfied with my job.   1   2   3   4   5
    (SKIP IF NOT WORKING)

n. I am very satisfied with motherhood.   1   2   3   4   5
    (SKIP IF NOT A MOTHER)

CONSEQUENCES OF NOT WORKING

15. This is the last time you will be asked to rate the items on this list. How likely is it
that each of these things might occur if you DID *NOT* WORK AT ALL DURING THE
FIRST THREE YEARS after the birth of your first child? (Circle one number for each
item. Answer hypothetically if you did work or have no child.)

CONSEQUENCES	EXTREMELY UNDESIRABLE				EXTREMELY DESIRABLE
HAVING FUN	1	2	3	4	5
A SENSE OF ACCOMPLISHMENT	1	2	3	4	5
FEELING TIED DOWN	1	2	3	4	5
HAVING VARIETY IN MY LIFE	1	2	3	4	5
FEELING GUILTY	1	2	3	4	5

FEELING RESENTFUL	1	2	3	4	5
FEELING TIRED	1	2	3	4	5
FEELING BORED	1	2	3	4	5
FEELING CLOSE TO MY HUSBAND	1	2	3	4	5
FEELING CLOSE TO MY CHILD	1	2	3	4	5
RUNNING MY HOUSEHOLD SMOOTHLY	1	2	3	4	5
TRAINING MY CHILD MYSELF	1	2	3	4	5
MAINTAINING MY CAREER SKILLS	1	2	3	4	5
MAINTAINING MY JOB CONTACTS	1	2	3	4	5
ADVANCING MY CAREER	1	2	3	4	5
EARNING ENOUGH INCOME MYSELF	1	2	3	4	5
HAVING ENOUGH FAMILY INCOME	1	2	3	4	5
HAVING EXTRA INCOME	1	2	3	4	5
MAKING MORE $ THAN IT COSTS ME TO WORK	1	2	3	4	5
HUSBAND NEEDING TWO JOBS	1	2	3	4	5
MISSING CHILD'S GROWTH MILESTONES	1	2	3	4	5
FINDING ADEQUATE CHILD CARE	1	2	3	4	5
HAVING ENOUGH TIME FOR THE CHILD	1	2	3	4	5
HAVING ENOUGH TIME FOR MYSELF	1	2	3	4	5
HAVING ENOUGH TIME FOR MY HUSBAND	1	2	3	4	5
HUSBAND HELPING AROUND THE HOUSE	1	2	3	4	5
CHILD WILL BE INDEPENDENT	1	2	3	4	5
CHILD WILL BE SECURE	1	2	3	4	5
CHILD WILL BE WELL DISCIPLINED	1	2	3	4	5
CHILD WILL GET ALONG EASILY WITH OTHERS	1	2	3	4	5
CHILD WILL DO BETTER IN SCHOOL	1	2	3	4	5
CHILD WILL FEEL LOVED	1	2	3	4	5
CHILD WILL HAVE ATTENTION WHEN NEEDED	1	2	3	4	5
CHILD FEELS CLOSER TO OTHERS THAN TO ME	1	2	3	4	5
CHILD WILL BELIEVE WOMEN ARE COMPETENT	1	2	3	4	5

INFLUENCE OF OTHERS

16. For many people, the opinions of their employers, parents, friends, or husband may be important in making decisions. Indicate how likely these people are to approve of your working during the first three years after childbirth. Also indicate how likely you are to do as they wish. (Circle two numbers for each person.) IF YOU HAVE NO PARTNER OR HUSBAND, SKIP THE QUESTIONS THAT APPLY TO HUSBANDS.

	VERY LIKELY TO DISAPPROVE		VERY LIKELY TO APPROVE			I AM LIKELY TO DO AS THEY WISH			I AM UNLIKELY TO DO AS THEY WISH	
a. Mother	1	2	3	4	5	1	2	3	4	5
b. Father	1	2	3	4	5	1	2	3	4	5
c. Husband	1	2	3	4	5	1	2	3	4	5
d. Best friend	1	2	3	4	5	1	2	3	4	5
e. Boss	1	2	3	4	5	1	2	3	4	5
f. Co-workers	1	2	3	4	5	1	2	3	4	5

17. If you have a spouse or partner, for the following questions please indicate the number that corresponds to your spouse's attitudes. IF YOU HAVE NOT YET HAD A CHILD, PLEASE ANSWER THE FIRST COLUMN. IF YOU HAVE HAD A CHILD, PLEASE ANSWER BOTH COLUMNS. IF NO PARTNER GO TO Q 8. The numbers are:

1	2	3	4	5
VERY NEGATIVE				VERY POSITIVE

	I Before the birth of your child	II After the birth of your child
a. How favorable is your spouse's attitude toward your career?	1 2 3 4 5	1 2 3 4 5
b. How much emotional support does your spouse provide in terms of your career?	1 2 3 4 5	1 2 3 4 5
c. How favorable are your spouse's feelings about your level of commitment to your career/professional work?	1 2 3 4 5	1 2 3 4 5

18. We would like you to describe your work history since leaving college. (PLEASE START WITH YOUR MOST RECENT JOB AND WORK BACK-WARD.) If you have ever been unemployed for more than four months since leaving college, please indicate the reasons for the breaks in employment and the length of time you were unemployed. Do not record jobs held for less than four months. If you need more room, use the inside front cover. Place an X beside the job you held before the birth of your first child.

Type of industry	Size of organization (Total # employees	Your occupation or unemployment	In terms of career, was change up, down, or lateral	Hours per week	Duration of employment or unemployment
1.					
2.					
3.					
4.					
5.					
6.					
7.					

19. If you have changed fields since college, why did you change?

20. Have you ever had to take a job that was a compromise? If so, why?

21. How likely is it that you will change careers in the next two to three years?

VERY UNLIKELY   VERY LIKELY

1   2   3   4   5

What is the most likely occupation that you would choose?

22. How likely are you to consider starting your own business as an alternative to finding another job?

VERY UNLIKELY   VERY LIKELY

1   2   3   4   5

What type of business would you start?

23. Next, we are interested in learning about the reasons why women might want to leave the organization for which they are employed, following birth of a child. With respect to your feelings about the *particular organization for which you worked immediately prior to the birth of your first child, or now if you have no child*, please circle one number for each item in this question.

	NOT AT ALL A FACTOR			DEFINITELY A FACTOR	
Opportunity to progress	5	4	3	2	1
Challenge of job	5	4	3	2	1
Wanted more time with child	5	4	3	2	1
Pressure from my spouse	5	4	3	2	1
Wanted to start my own business	5	4	3	2	1
Bored with routine	5	4	3	2	1
Long hours on the job	5	4	3	2	1
Amount of travel	5	4	3	2	1
Sexual harassment	5	4	3	2	1
Conflict between work and family	5	4	3	2	1
Inflexible work hours	5	4	3	2	1
Relationship with boss	5	4	3	2	1
Child care availability	5	4	3	2	1
Disliked working in a male-dominated environment	5	4	3	2	1
Pay inequity	5	4	3	2	1
Compatibility with co-workers	5	4	3	2	1
Lack of career guidance or mentor	5	4	3	2	1
Office politics	5	4	3	2	1
Competent child care	5	4	3	2	1
% of female co-workers	5	4	3	2	1
Sexual discrimination	5	4	3	2	1

24. Please indicate the degree of your agreement or disagreement by circling one of the alternatives below for each question.

	STRONGLY DISAGREE			STRONGLY AGREE	
a. I am willing to put in a great deal of effort beyond that normally expected in order to help this organization be successful.	5	4	3	2	1

	STRONGLY DISAGREE			STRONGLY AGREE	
b. Often I find it difficult to agree with the organization's values.	5	4	3	2	1
c. I am proud to tell others that I am part of this organization.	5	4	3	2	1
d. It would take very little change in my present circumstances to cause me to leave this organization.	5	4	3	2	1
e. I feel that there's not too much to be gained by sticking with this organization.	5	4	3	2	1

25. Looking back over your jobs up to the birth of your child, or now if you have not yet had a child, please indicate the extent to which your expectations in the areas listed below were (are) met.

	GREATLY EXCEEDED MY EXPECTATIONS			HAS NOT LIVED UP TO MY EXPECTATIONS	
Salary	5	4	3	2	1
Career advancement	5	4	3	2	1
Stress	5	4	3	2	1
Hours required	5	4	3	2	1
Status	5	4	3	2	1
Ability to develop new skills	5	4	3	2	1
Good working conditions	5	4	3	2	1
Interesting work	5	4	3	2	1
Responsibility	5	4	3	2	1
Variety	5	4	3	2	1
Autonomy (independence)	5	4	3	2	1
Challenge	5	4	3	2	1
Leadership	5	4	3	2	1
Clarity about what I should do	5	4	3	2	1

IF YOU DO NOT HAVE A CHILD, PLEASE GO TO THE LAST PAGE OF THE QUESTIONNAIRE NOW. IF YOU HAVE A CHILD, PLEASE CONTINUE.

26. Thinking back to the birth of your first child, to what extent would you have agreed or disagreed with each of the following statements? Please circle the number which best corresponds to your views.

	STRONGLY DISAGREE			STRONGLY AGREE
a. More than any other adult, I can meet my child's needs best.	5	4	3	2	1
b. My child is happier with me than with baby sitters or teachers.	5	4	3	2	1
c. I am naturally better at keeping my child safe than any other person.	5	4	3	2	1
d. It is not good for my child to be cared for by someone else because he/she may be exposed to values and attitudes with which I disagree.	5	4	3	2	1
e. Only a mother just naturally knows how to comfort her distressed child.	5	4	3	2	1

27. How satisfied were you with your job overall?

1   2   3   4   5

VERY DISSATISFIED   VERY SATISFIED

28. To what extent were you considering quitting?

1   2   3   4   5

NEVER THOUGHT ABOUT IT   FREQUENTLY THOUGHT ABOUT IT

29. To what extent did you consider looking for another job?

1   2   3   4   5

NEVER THOUGHT ABOUT IT   FREQUENTLY THOUGHT ABOUT IT

30. How extensively did you look for another job?

1   2   3   4   5

NOT AT ALL   A GREAT DEAL

31. What did you think was the likelihood you could have found an acceptable alternative with another company?

1   2   3   4   5

VERY UNLIKELY   VERY LIKELY

32. What did you think was the probability you could have or adopt a child at the time you wanted to?

1	2	3	4	5

VERY UNLIKELY   VERY LIKELY

33. How likely were you to consider homemaking as an alternative to finding another job?

1	2	3	4	5

VERY UNLIKELY   VERY LIKELY

34. To what extent was your pregnancy (adoption) planned?

1	2	3	4	5

NOT AT ALL   A GREAT DEAL

35. How flexible was your work schedule?

1	2	3	4	5

VERY INFLEXIBLE   VERY FLEXIBLE

36. How much travel did your job require?

1	2	3	4	5

VERY LITTLE   VERY MUCH

37. When people such as yourself think about child care arrangements, they have three frequent concerns: availability, affordability, and quality. How much of a problem was each issue in your decision about suitable child care arrangements?

	NOT AT ALL A PROBLEM			MAJOR PROBLEM	
1. *Availability*	5	4	3	2	1
2. *Affordability*	5	4	3	2	1
3. *Quality*	5	4	3	2	1

38. Did your employer prior to the birth of your first child provide any type of child care benefits? Please check all that apply.

_____ On or near site child care _____ Other

_____ Information and referral services _____ Financial assistance

_____ Not employed

39. Please indicate how many *months* you used each of the following child care arrangements between the birth of your first child and the present. Answer for all alternatives used.

_____ I did not return to work and am the primary caretaker of my child (GO TO Q 42)

_____ My child was in a day care center

_____ My child was cared for by a relative (other than spouse)

_____ My spouse cared for our child

_____ My child was in a group day care in someone's home

_____ I had a baby sitter care for my child in our home

_____ I had live-in help to care for my child

_____ Other_____

40. Do you worry when you leave your child with someone else? (Please circle)

NOT AT ALL	VERY LITTLE	SOMEWHAT	A MODERATE AMOUNT	QUITE A BIT
1	2	3	4	5

41. Overall, how satisfied are/were you with your child care arrangements at the time you returned to work? (Circle the best response)

VERY SATISFIED				VERY DISSATISFIED
1	2	3	4	5

42. Please circle one response for each item.

	STRONGLY DISAGREE			STRONGLY AGREE	
1. I am willing to put in a great deal of effort beyond that normally expected in order to be successful as a homemaker.	5	4	3	2	1
2. I would do almost anything to remain a homemaker.	5	4	3	2	1
3. I am proud to tell others I am a homemaker.	5	4	3	2	1
4. It would take very little in my present circumstances to get me to become an employed mother. (SKIP IF WORKING)	5	4	3	2	1
5. I feel that there is not too much to be gained from remaining a homemaker.	5	4	3	2	1
6. Often I find it difficult to agree with the values espoused by homemakers.	5	4	3	2	1
7. To me being a homemaker is the best of all possible roles to hold.	5	4	3	2	1

43. If you had adequate child care arrangements, how likely is it that you would have returned to work shortly after the birth of your child?

VERY LIKELY	SOMEWHAT LIKELY	HAVE NO EFFECT	SOMEWHAT UNLIKELY	VERY UNLIKELY
5	4	3	2	1

PART F—BACKGROUND INFORMATION

44. What is the highest level of regular school that you have ever attained?
_____ a. Graduated from a four-year college.
_____ b. Some postgraduate work.
_____ c. Obtained a Master's degree.
_____ d. Obtained a terminal degree (e.g., M.D., LLD., Ph.D.)

45. What is your current marital status?
_____ a. Not in a long-term relationship.
_____ b. In a long-term relationship or engaged.
_____ c. Married.
_____ d. Separated or divorced.

46. If you are currently married or living with a partner, what is your mate's occupation?

47. On average, how many hours per week does he work?

48. How flexible is his schedule?   Very Inflexible   Very Flexible
                                        1   2   3   4   5

49. What are your own and your mate's current gross annual incomes from all sources at this time? Make one X in *each* column opposite the approximate amount.

	Self	Spouse
Less than $20,000		
20,000–29,000		
30,000–39,000		
40,000–49,000		
50,000–59,000		
60,000–69,000		
70,000–79,000		
80,000 and up		

Thank you for taking the time to answer this questionnaire. Please put the booklet *and the permission letter* in the envelope provided and return it to us via U.S. Mail.

TELEPHONE INTERVIEW PROTOCOL

(Forms A, Nonmothers; B, Homemakers; and C, Working Mothers; Combined)

DESCRIPTION OF STUDY & INTERVIEW

Let me just briefly go over what the study is about and what the interview involves. As you already know, we're interested in women's decisions to return to work after childbirth and the factors that influenced that decision. Note: Work is defined as ten hours or more per week of paid work.

In particular, we'd like to know more about some of the satisfactions and challenges women experience in their careers and families as well as in combining the two. The interview will take about thirty minutes.

I. GENERAL QUESTIONS/BACKGROUND

1. When you were in college did you expect to go back to work within three years after having a baby? _____ Yes _____ No

   Did your plans change? _____ Yes

   _____ No

   _____ Don't remember

   If yes, interviewer checks one.

   _____ Expected to stay home, but will return to work (10 or more hours per week—paid work).

   _____ Expected to return to work, but will stay home with child.

2. If yes: Why did they change?

    Probe: Be more specific about work experiences and things at home that changed your plans.

    If no: Why didn't they change?

II. WORK SITUATION

Next, we'd like to ask you a few questions about your job before you gave birth. [All]

3. What kind of job did you have just before you gave birth?

    Probes: What did you actually do on the job?

    What was your position?

    What kind of business/industry was it?

4. Are you on a leave of absence from your job or did you leave your job permanently?

5. If respondent is not working outside the home:

    Did you attempt to negotiate a professional part-time position before leaving your previous employer?

    If so, what were your employer's objections?

6. Have your thoughts about combining work and family changed since you had the child?

    _____ Yes

    _____ No

    If they have changed, ask why and how.

7. What are your plans now? Do you plan to work again?

    Probes: Facilitators/Motivators

    Constraints/Barriers

7a. When your child is how old? (Note: Determine—is R returning within three years of birth or after?)

8. What will be your main reason for going back to work?

    If R gives financial reason, ask: Would you work if you had enough money to live comfortably?)

9. How difficult do you think it will be to get a job as good as the one you had before the birth of your child?

    Probe: Why?

10. Now that you are staying home, do you have a career goal? If so, what is it? [Homemakers only]

III. CAREER PLANS

11. What job do you *ultimately* aspire to? [All]

    (How would that differ from current job, re: time, responsibility, etc.?) [Working women only]

12. Do you have any particular strategy for reaching that goal? [All]

13. Looking back, what would you have done differently?

    Probes: Would you have planned more in the past?

    Will you plan more in the future?

14. How far into the future does your career plan extend?

    What would you say are your career plans for the future?

    Probes: One day at a time

    The next year

    2–5 years

    6–10 years

    More than 10 years

IV. MOBILITY

15. Can you tell us something about your job now?

    Probes: What do you actually do on the job?

    What is your position?

    What type of business/industry is it?

16. Are you satisfied with your rate of progress in your career/job?

    How would you compare your rate of progress to:

    Probes: Others in your industry/job/occupation?

    Male peers?

V. DESCRIPTION OF WORK/ORG. CLIMATE

17. How would you describe morale in your company?

    Probes: Is the atmosphere relaxed or tense?

    Are there many complaints; if so what about?

    (Anything unusual in past years—layoffs, mergers, budget cuts?)

18. Stress/Pressure

    All of us encounter stress on the job. Could you describe a particular incident or situation at work that was stressful for you?

    Probes: Time demands

    Take home work

    Work weekends

    Deadlines

    Poor training

19. Does stress on the job "spill over" into your personal (family) life? How do you feel with these situations?

20. What is the attitude/climate toward women?

    Probes: % women in dept. in which you work

        Informal networks

        Sexual harassment

        % of women in senior mgmt. levels

        Leaves for pregnancy

20a. Can you tell us about a situation where this has been an issue?

21. What would you say is the attitude in your organization toward individuals who combine work and family?

    How is this expressed?

    Formally

    Informally

    (Can you describe an incident where this policy was expressed?)

22. Does your company have policies designed for working parents?

    Probes: Child care services

        Work at home

        Job-sharing

        Other

    If no, can you tell us why?

23. Is there anything in your organization (e.g., a policy) that has facilitated or constrained your going back to work?

24. How has your involvement with your job and career increased or decreased since you became a mother? What do you think caused it?

    Can you tell us about a situation where this has been evident to you?

25. From *your company's* point of view, has your career been affected since you had your child?

26. Do you work part-time? _____ Yes   _____ No

    If yes, approximately how many hours per week?

26a. Did you propose part-time work? Is part-time work an option offered to all employees (including professionals), or is it offered only on a case-by-case basis? What do you see as the disadvantages of working part time, from a career standpoint?

    Next, we would like to ask you a few questions about your personal life.

V. PERSONAL LIFE AND/OR FAMILY

27. Do you have a spouse or long-term relationship?

28. What does your partner do?

29. In what ways do you feel that your partner's work *helps* and/or *hinders* your work? Can you give an example?

    Probes: help around house

      work long hours

      support

30. How does your partner feel about your returning to work if you have a child? Can you tell us something about why he feels this way?

    How does he feel about your working (not working) while the child is young?

VI. EMOTIONAL SUPPORT AND COPING

31. When you feel like talking about your concerns about work or personal life, whom do you talk to?

    Can you describe or give an example of such a situation?

32. Are there any role models—either in your personal life or at work—who are helpful to you? In what ways?

33. What do you do for yourself to cope with your busy schedule?

    Next, we would like to ask you some questions about becoming a mother.

VII. BECOMING A MOTHER [Mothers only]

34. *(Expectations vs. reality)*

    Many women say that being a mother is different from what they expected. How has your experience as a mother compared to what you thought it would be like? (IF DIFFERENT, ASK: In what ways?)

35. *(How baby changes life)*

    How would you say your life has changed as a result of having a baby?

36. Is there anything else in your family life that facilitates or hinders your working? [Working mothers only]

    Can you give us an example?

37. What kind of child care arrangements do you have?

38. Some women have told us that they wouldn't leave their job because of their child care arrangements (e.g., on-site). Have your child care arrangements ever affected/hindered your career (plans) in any way?

39. Have/How often do your child care arrangements affect(ed) your performance on the job?

    Can you describe a situation where this was a problem?

40. Is there anything you would like to ask us?

    Thank you for your time.

TABLES COMPARING FOUR GROUPS OF WOMEN

Table A.1
Description of Participants: Family, Education, and Employment

Phase I[a]	Careerists	Homemakers	Breadwinners	Nesters
Mother Employed When				
Subject's Age Was[*]				
Birth-3 years	29.2	11.5	13.0	13.4
3-5 years	43.2	20.4	17.1	37.5
6-12 years	59.5	42.6	41.4	62.5
> 13	78.4	64.8	71.4	75.0
Religion				
Protestant	17.6	25.5	21.4	18.8
Catholic	41.9	49.1	42.9	56.3
Jewish	23.0	12.7	18.6	12.5
Other	17.6	12.8	17.1	12.6
Residence Growing Up[*]				
Country	5.5	10.9	5.6	18.8
Town/small city	74.0	74.5	84.5	37.5
Large city (> 100,000)	20.5	14.5	9.9	43.8
Average Age in Years	20.9	20.6	20.7	20.7
Birth Order[*]	1.9	2.5	2.0	2.1
Race				
Black	6.5	3.6	4.2	12.6
White	93.5	96.4	95.8	87.4
Mother's Nationality				
U.S.	87.5	90.9	91.2	86.7
Other than U.S.	12.5	9.1	8.8	13.3

Table A.1 (Continued)

Phase I	Careerists	Homemakers	Breadwinners	Nesters
Father's Nationality				
U.S.	16.4	14.5	10.0	12.5
Other than U.S.	83.6	85.5	90.0	87.5
Mother's Education				
High school	60.5	67.3	54.3	66.7
Some college	17.4	14.5	17.7	13.4
College graduate	12.7	14.5	23.5	13.3
Postgraduate	8.4	3.6	4.4	6.7
Father's Education⁻				
High school	54.9	63.6	31.4	62.7
Some college	12.3	3.6	18.6	---
College graduate	17.8	16.4	34.3	12.5
Postgraduate	15.1	3.6	15.7	25.0
Own Marital Status				
No relationship	43.2	49.1	45.1	56.3
Going steady	32.4	29.1	36.6	25.0
Living in/Engaged	18.9	21.8	14.1	18.8
Married	4.1	---	2.8	---
Divorced	1.4	---	1.4	---
Industry of College Job				
Manufacturing	9.1	14.3	10.2	16.7
Wholesale/retail trade	9.1	2.4	4.1	---
Finance and insurance	12.7	16.7	28.6	25.0
Service industry	65.5	59.5	44.9	58.3
Public administration	3.6	7.1	8.2	---

Table A.1 (Continued)

Phase I	Careerists	Homemakers	Breadwinners	Nesters
Occupation of College Job				
Service	82.4	69.8	74.4	74.9
Science and technology	---	3.8	4.2	---
Business	17.6	24.5	21.4	25.1
Duration of College Work				
< 2 months	12.3	17.0	16.9	25.1
3-5 months	28.7	24.5	22.5	37.6
6-12 months	12.3	13.3	18.3	6.3
> 12 months	46.7	45.2	42.3	31.0
Hours/Week of College Job				
Below 35 hours	82.1	77.3	87.4	87.4
35 hours and above	17.9	22.7	12.6	12.6
Phase II				
Education*				
BS	46.7	68.5	59.2	66.7
MS	40.0	27.8	33.8	26.7
MD/PhD/LLD	13.3	3.7	7.0	6.7
Marital Status				
Single	13.3	18.5	8.5	18.8
Married/relationship	86.7	79.6	90.1	75.1
Divorced/Widowed	---	1.9	1.4	6.3
Industry of First Postcollege Job (Job 1)				
Manufacturing	9.1	14.3	10.2	16.7
Wholesale/retail trade	9.1	2.4	4.1	---
Finance and insurance	12.7	16.7	28.6	25.0
Service industry	65.5	59.5	44.9	58.3
Public administration	3.6	7.1	8.2	---

Table A.1 (Continued)

Phase II	Careerists	Homemakers	Breadwinners	Nesters
Occupation of Job 1*				
Service	21.9	20.8	27.7	7.7
Arts	6.3	4.2	3.2	---
Science and technology	12.5	6.3	11.1	7.7
Business	34.4	50.0	41.1	53.8
Medicine, Law	23.4	4.1	15.8	7.7
Housewife	1.6	14.6	---	---
Organization Size of Job 1				
< 100	36.5	22.6	36.9	54.5
100-500	23.8	27.3	15.4	18.2
500-1000	6.3	11.4	6.2	---
1000-5000	17.5	18.2	24.6	18.2
> 5000	15.9	20.5	16.9	9.1
Duration of Job 1*				
< 2 years	60.2	80.0	46.3	66.7
3-5 years	30.1	6.7	34.8	22.3
6-10 years	8.3	13.3	17.5	9.3
> 10 years	1.4	---	1.4	1.9
Hours/Week of Job 1				
Below 35 hours	19.2	27.2	20.0	---
More than 35 hours	80.8	72.8	80.0	100.0

Table A.1 (Continued)

Phase II	Careerists	Homemakers	Breadwinners	Nesters
Career Change Job 1 to Job 2*				
Down	8.8	5.6	7.9	---
Lateral	22.1	22.2	20.6	54.5
Up	69.1	69.4	71.4	45.5
Job Held at Childbirth*				
Manufacturing, mining,				
construction	6.8	21.9	13.2	---
Wholesale/retail trade	4.5	6.3	---	---
Finance, insurance and				
real estate	13.6	21.9	31.6	25.0
Service industries	70.5	46.9	50.0	43.8
Public administration	4.5	3.1	---	---
Occupation at Childbirth*				
Service	21.9	20.8	28.5	7.7
Arts	6.3	4.2	3.2	---
Science and technology	12.5	6.3	11.1	7.7
Business	34.4	50.0	41.3	53.8
Medicine, law	23.4	4.2	15.8	7.7
Housewife	1.6	14.6	---	7.7
Hours/Week, Job at Childbirth*				
35 hours	19.2	27.2	20.0	---
More than 35 hours	80.8	72.8	80.0	100.0
Job Tenure at Childbirth				
< 2 years	45.4	66.7	47.4	75.1
3-5 years	30.7	22.3	33.8	6.3
6-10 years	7.9	9.3	16.8	12.5
> 10 years	1.3	1.9	1.4	6.3

Table A.1 (Continued)

Phase II	Careerists	Homemakers	Breadwinners	Nesters
Own Current Income[*],[b]				
< 20K	22.5	44.4	20.3	40.0
20-29K	15.5	15.6	18.8	20.0
30-39K	32.4	24.4	33.3	26.7
40-49K	14.1	6.7	13.0	13.3
50-59K	11.3	---	4.3	---
60-69K	2.8	6.7	2.9	---
70-79K	---	---	4.3	---
> 80K	---	---	4.3	---
Husband's Income				
< 20K	4.8	5.0	6.7	11.1
20-29K	9.7	15.0	11.7	11.1
30-39K	16.1	5.0	18.3	22.2
40-49K	27.4	22.5	21.7	---
50-59K	17.1	25.0	8.3	11.1
60-69K	8.1	2.5	8.3	11.1
70-79K	4.8	2.5	3.3	11.1
> 80K	11.3	22.5	11.7	22.2
Husband's Hours/Week[*]				
< 35 hours	6.5	2.4	5.1	---
> 35 hours	93.5	97.6	94.9	100.0

*Groups are significantly different, $p \leq .05$
[a]All number are %; totals may not equal 100% due to rounding or no response.
[b]Current income of Homemakers and Nesters was for nonmothers.

Table A.2
Phase II Met Employment Expectations of All Participants

	Careerists	Homemakers	Breadwinners	Nesters
Salary[e]	2.86[c]	2.83[c]	3.34[a,b,d]	2.38[c]
Career advancement	3.11	3.02	3.30[d]	2.62[c]
Stress	3.45	3.56	3.61	3.50
Hours required	3.37	3.54	3.54	3.38
Status	3.12	3.11	3.31	2.94
Develop new skills	3.47	3.37	3.46	3.50
Working conditions	3.49	3.32	3.46	3.25
Interesting work	3.68	3.57	3.61	3.44
Responsibility	3.90	3.78	3.82	3.81
Variety	3.74	3.43	3.58	3.44
Autonomy	3.67	3.63	3.76	3.56
Challenge	3.83	3.61	3.72	3.44
Leadership	3.40[d]	3.44[d]	3.41[d]	2.94[a,b,c]
Clarity about what to do	3.24[d]	3.20[d]	3.22[d]	2.94[a,b,c]

[a]Significantly different from Careerists, $p > .05$
[b]Significantly different from Homemakers, $p > .05$
[c]Significantly different from Breadwinners, $p > .05$
[d]Significantly different from Nesters, $p > .05$
[e]1–Has not lived up to my expectations, 5–Greatly exceeded my expectations.

Table A.3

Phase II Factors Encouraging All Participants to Leave an Organization

	Careerists	Homemakers	Breadwinners	Nesters
Opportunity to progress[e]	3.73[b]	2.77[a,b]	3.56	3.69[b]
Challenge of job	3.57	3.09	3.52	3.56
Wanted more time with child	4.20[b]	4.74[a]	4.62	4.56
Pressure from my spouse	2.64	3.04	2.64	3.33
Wanted to start my				
own business	2.47	2.45	2.26	2.19
Bored with routine	3.27	3.06	3.02	3.12
Long hours on the job	3.65	3.85	2.21	3.00
Amount of travel	2.93	2.50	2.97	3.12
Sexual harassment	2.32	1.68	2.18	2.69
Conflict between work				
and family	3.57	3.92	3.83	4.38
Inflexible work hours	3.39	2.65	3.47	3.62
Relationship with boss	3.05	2.67	2.76	3.31
Childcare availability	3.93	4.10	3.86	3.94
Disliked male-dominated				
environment	2.09	2.04	1.73	2.12
Pay inequity	2.81	2.61	2.67	3.31
Compatibility with				
co-workers	2.59	2.06	2.35	2.62
Lack of career guidance				
or mentor	2.49	2.48	2.39	3.25
Office politics	2.75	2.46	2.74	3.06
Competent childcare	4.01	3.89	3.83	3.69
% of female co-workers	1.89	1.80	1.47	1.94
Sexual discrimination	2.53	2.00	2.14	2.62

[a]Significantly different from Careerists, $p > .05$
[b]Significantly different from Homemakers, $p > .05$
[c]Significantly different from Breadwinners, $p > .05$
[d]Significantly different from Nesters, $p > .05$
[e]5–Definitely a factor, 1–not at all a factor (reversed from the questionnaire)

Table A.4
Phase II Commitment to Maternal Care and Homemaking

	Careerists	Homemakers	Breadwinners	Nesters
More than any other adult, I can meet my child's needs best.	4.17	4.80	4.25	4.40
My child is happier with me than with baby sitters or teachers.	3.64	4.39	4.11	4.20
I am naturally better at keeping my child safe than any other person.	3.56	3.46	3.54	4.20
It is not good for my child to be cared for by someone else because he/she may be exposed to values and attitudes with which I disagree.	2.42	3.07	3.00	2.80
Only a mother just naturally knows how to comfort her distressed child.	2.56	2.93	2.83	2.80
I am willing to put in a great deal of effort beyond that normally expected in order to be successful as a homemaker.	3.17	3.78	3.34	3.80
I would do almost anything to remain a homemaker.	2.22	3.22	2.58	2.40
I am proud to tell others I am a homemaker.	2.75[b]	3.63[a]	2.77	3.40

Table A. 4 (Continued)

	Careerists	Homemakers	Breadwinners	Nesters
It would take very little in my present circumstances to get me to become an employed mother (SKIP IF WORKING).	---	1.79	---	3.00
I feel that there is not too much to be gained by remaining a homemaker.	2.53[b]	1.70[a]	2.31	2.40
Often I find it difficult to agree with the values espoused by homemakers.	2.69	1.92	2.75	3.20
To me being a homemaker is the best of all possible roles to hold.	2.28[b]	3.37[a]	2.77	2.40

[a]Significantly different from Careerists, $p > .05$
[b]Significantly different from Homemakers, $p > .05$
[c]Significantly different from Breadwinners, $p > .05$
[d]Significantly different from Nesters, $p > .05$
[e]1–strongly disagree, 5–strongly agree (reversed from the questionnaire)

Table A.5
Phase II Competence and Self-Confidence

	Careerists	Homemakers	Breadwinners	Nesters
I feel that I'm a person of worth at least on an equal basis with others.	4.78[d]	4.74[d]	4.79[d]	4.31[a,b,c]
I am able to do things as well as most other people	4.66	4.62	4.62	3.88
I certainly feel useless at times.	2.57	2.53	2.49	2.75
Problems are easy to solve once you understand the various consequences of your actions.	3.64	3.74	3.55	3.56

Table A5. (Continued)

	Careerists	Homemakers	Breadwinners	Nesters
I would make a fine model for an apprentice to learn the skills she/he would need to succeed.	3.64	3.74	3.61	3.56
If anyone can find the answer, I'm the one.	3.45	3.42	3.25	3.69
My talents, or where I can concentrate my attention best, are found in areas not related to this job.	2.51	2.80	2.76	2.81
Mastering my job doesn't mean much to me.	1.73	1.80	1.99	1.94
It is important to me to be seen by others as very successful.	3.40	3.31	3.37	3.44
I very badly want to "make my mark" in my career.	3.27[b]	2.66[a]	3.11	3.13

[a]Significantly different from Careerists, $p > .05$
[b]Significantly different from Homemakers, $p > .05$
[c]Significantly different from Breadwinners, $p > .05$
[d]Significantly different from Nesters, $p > .05$
[e]1–strongly disagree, 5–strongly agree (reversed from the questionnaire)

Selected Bibliography

Almquist, E. M., Angrist, S. S., & Mickelson, R. (1980). Women's career aspirations and achievements: College and seven years after. *Sociology of Work and Occupations*, *7*, 367–384.

Angrist, S. S., & Almquist, E. M. (1975). *Careers and contingencies*. New York: Dunellen.

Arthur, M. B., Hall, D. T., & Lawrence, B. S. (1989). *Handbook of career theory*. Cambridge, Eng.: Cambridge University Press.

Baruch, G., Barnett, R., & Rivers, C. (1983). *Lifeprints: New patterns of love and work for today's women*. New York: Signet.

Berk, S. F. (1985). *The gender factory: The apportionment of work in American households*. New York: Plenum.

Bielby, D. D., & Bielby, W. T. (1988). Women's and men's commitment to paid work and family. In B. A. Gutek, A. H. Stromberg, & L. Larwood (Eds.), *Women and work*, vol. 3, pp. 249–263. Newbury Park, CA: Sage.

Bielby, D. D., & Bielby, W. T. (1984). Work commitment, sex role attitudes, and women's employment. *American Sociological Review*, *49*, 234–347.

Brenner, O. C. (1988). Relations of age and education to managers' work values. *Psychological Reports*, *63*, 639–642.

Covin, T. J., & Brush, C. C. (1991). An examination of male and female attitudes toward career and family issues. *Sex Roles*, *25*, 393–415.

Crosby, F. J. (1991). *Juggling: The unexpected advantages of balancing career and home for women and their families*. New York: The Free Press.

Crosby, F. J. (Ed.). (1987). *Spouse, parent, worker*. New Haven, CT: Yale University Press.

Drucker, P. F. (1988, Jan.–Feb.). The coming of the new organization. *Harvard Business Review*, 65–76.

Erikson, E. (1980). *Identity and the life cycle*. New York: Norton.

Gardels, N. (Ed.). (1990). Prodigal parents: Family vs. the 80-hour work week. *New Perspectives Quarterly, 7*, whole issue.

Gerson, K. (1985). *Hard choices: How women decide about work, career and motherhood*. Berkeley: University of California Press.

Gilbert, L. A. (1994). Current perspectives on dual-career families. *American Psychologist, 3*, 101–105.

Gilligan, C. (1982). *In a different voice: Psychological theory and women's development*. Cambridge, MA: Harvard University Press.

Granrose, C. S., & Portwood, J. D. (1987). Matching individual career plans and organizational career management. *Academy of Management Journal, 30*(4), 699–720.

Griffin, M. A., & Mathieu, J. E. (1993). *The role of comparisons in turnover related processes*. Paper presented at Academy of Management Meeting, Atlanta, GA.

Hall, D. T., & Richter, J. (1992). Career gridlock: Baby boomers hit the wall. *Academy of Management Executive, 4*, 7–22.

Helson, R., & Picano, J. (1990). Is the traditional role bad for women? *Journal of Personality and Social Psychology, 59*, 311–320.

Hennig, M., & Jardin, A. (1977). *The managerial woman*. Garden City, NY: Anchor Press/Doubleday.

Hisrich, R. D., & Brush, C. G. (1986). *The woman entrepreneur*. Lexington, MA: Lexington Books.

Hulbert, K. D., & Schuster, D. T. (Eds.). (1994). *Women's lives through time*. San Francisco: Jossey Bass.

Jenkins, S. R. (1987). Need for achievement and women's careers over 14 years: Evidence for occupational structure effects. *Journal of Personality and Social Psychology, 53*, 922–932.

Jick, T. D. (1985). As the ax falls: Budget cuts and the experience of stress in organizations. In T. A. Beehr & R. S. Bhagat (Eds.), *Human stress and cognition in organizations*. New York: Wiley.

Kimmel, J. (1992). *Child care and the employment behavior of single and married mothers*. Kalamazoo, MI: W. E. Upjohn Institute, Staff Working Papers, 92–14.

Kirchmeyer, C. (1993). Nonwork-to-work spillover: A more balanced view of the experiences and coping of professional women and men. *Sex Roles, 28*, 531–552.

Landy, M. (1990). *Planning positive careers*. Englewood Cliffs, NJ: Prentice Hall.

Larwood, L., & Gattiker, U. E. (1987). A comparison of the career paths used by successful women and men. In B. A. Gutek & L. Larwood (Eds.), *Women's career development*, pp. 129–156. Beverly Hills, CA: Sage.

Larwood, L., & Gutek, B. A. (1987). Working toward a theory of women's career development. In B. A. Gutek & L. Larwood (Eds.), *Women's Career Development*, pp. 170–183. Beverly Hills, CA: Sage.

Lerner, J. V., & Galambos, N. L. 1991. *Employed mothers and their children*. New York: Garland.

Levinson, D. (1978). *The seasons of a man's life*. New York: Ballantine.

Lueptow, L. B. (1985). Conceptions of femininity and masculinity: 1974–1983. *Psychological Reports, 57*, 859–862.

Miller, G., Galanter, E., & Pribram, K. (1960). *Plans and the structure of behavior*. New York: Holt, Rinehart and Winston.

Miller, J. G., & Wheeler, K. G. (1992). Unraveling the mysteries of gender differences in intentions to leave the organization. *Journal of Organizational Behavior, 13*, 465–478.

Morgan, E., & Farber, B. A. (1982). Toward a re-formulation of the Ericksonian model of female identity development. *Adolescence, 17*, 199–211.

Morrison, A. M., White, R. P., & Van Velsor, E. V. (1987). *Breaking the glass ceiling: Can women reach the top of America's largest corporations?* Reading, MA: Addison Wesley.

Ornstein, S., & Isabella, L. (1990). Age vs. stage models of career attitudes of women: A partial replication and extension. *Journal of Vocational Behavior, 36*, 1–19.

Parker, B., & Chusmir, L. (1990). A generational and sex-based view of managerial work values. *Psychological Reports, 66*, 947–950.

Powell, G. N., & Mainiero, L. A. (1992). Cross-currents in the river of time: Conceptualizing the complexities of women's careers. *Journal of Management, 18*, 215–237.

Reinke, B. J., Holmes, D. S., & Harris, R. L. (1985). The timing of psychosocial changes in women's lives: The years 25 to 45. *Journal of Personality and Social Psychology, 48*, 1353–1364.

Rexroat, C. (1992). Changes in the employment continuity of succeeding cohorts of young women. *Work and Occupations, 19*(1), 18–34.

Rix, S. E. (Ed.). (1990). *The American woman 1988–89: A status report*. New York: W. W. Norton & Co.

Schneer, J. A., & Reitman, F. (1993). Effects of alternate family structures on managerial career paths. *Academy of Management Journal, 36*, 830–843.

Schwartz, F. (1989, Jan.–Feb.). Management women and the new facts of life. *Harvard Business Review*, 65–76.

Simon, H. (1978). Rationality as a process and as product of thought. *American Economic Review, 68*, 1–16.

Stewart, A. J. (1978). A longitudinal study of coping styles of self-defining and socially defined women. *Journal of Consulting and Clinical Psychology, 46*, 1079–1084.

Stewart, A. J., & Healy, J. M., Jr. (1989). Linking individual development and social changes. *American Psychologist, 44*, 30–42.

Stewart, A. J., & Vandewater, E. A. (1994). The Radcliffe class of 1964: Career and family social clock projects in a transitional cohort. In K. D. Hulbert & D. T. Schuster (Eds.), *Women's lives through time*, 235–258. San Francisco: Jossey Bass.

Stroh, L. K., Brett, J. M., & Reilly, A. H. (1992). All the right stuff: A comparison of female and male managers' career progression. *Journal of Applied Psychology, 77*, 251–260.

Tangri, S. S., & Jenkins, S. R. (1986). Stability and change in role innovation and life plans. *Sex Roles, 14*, 647–662.

U.S. Department of Labor. (1991). *A report on the glass ceiling initiative.* Washington, DC: U.S. Department of Labor, Lynn Martin, Secretary.

U.S. Department of Labor. (1994). *Working women count: A report to the nation.* Washington, DC: U.S. Department of Labor, Women's Bureau, Karen Nussbaum, Director.

Vodanovich, S. J., & Kramer, T. J. (1989). An examination of the work values of parents and their children. *The Career Development Quarterly, 37*, 365–374.

Voydanoff, P. (1988). Work and family: A review and expanded conceptualization. *Journal of Social Behavior and Personality, 3*, 1–22.

Whisler, S. C., & Eklund, S. J. (1986). Women's ambitions: A three-generational study. *Psychology of Women Quarterly, 10*, 353–362.

Zajonc, R. B., & Markus, G. B. (1975). Birth order and intellectual development. *Psychological Review, 82*, 74–88.

Index

About the Authors

CHERLYN SKROMME GRANROSE is currently Professor of Organizational Behavior at Claremont Graduate School. She received her Ph.D. in psychology from Rutgers University. For 13 years she taught organizational behavior and human resources at Temple University.

EILEEN E. KAPLAN is Professor of Management at Montclair State University where she teaches Human Resource Management. She received her Ph.D. in psychology from Rutgers University.

ISBN 0-275-95525-7

HARDCOVER BAR CODE